Scenarios in Business

Scenarios in Business

Gill Ringland

JOHN WILEY & SONS LTD

Other Wiley Editorial Offices

John Wiley & Sons, Inc., 605 Third Avenue,
New York, NY 10158-0012, USA

Wiley-VCH Verlag GmbH, Pappelallee 3,
D-69469 Weinheim, Germany

John Wiley & Sons Australia Ltd., 33 Park Road, Milton,
Queensland 4064, Australia

John Wiley & Sons (Asia) Pte Ltd, 2 Clementi Loop #02-01,
Jin Xing Distripark, Singapore 129809

John Wiley & Sons (Canada) Ltd, 22 Worcester Road,
Rexdale, Ontario M9W 1L1, Canada

British Library Cataloguing in Publication Data
A catalogue record for this book is available from the British Library

ISBN 0-470-84382-9

Project management by Originator, Gt Yarmouth (typeset in 11/13pt Garamond)
Printed and bound in Great Britain by TJ International Ltd, Padstow, Cornwall
This book is printed on acid-free paper responsibly manufactured from sustainable forestry,
in which at least two trees are planted for each one used for paper production.

Contents

Contents

About the author

Gill Ringland graduated as a physicist, spending two years at the University of California at Berkeley and a year as a Fellow at Oxford. After working for an expanding computer software house, a start-up, and a US company, Gill built a number of businesses inside ICL before becoming Group Executive responsible for strategy. She then started The Lifestyle Network – to study the changes in consumer lifestyles, now adopted by the Cranfield School of Management as part of their New Marketing Research Club. She has worked with a number of organizations on strategic issues, focusing on future-resilient decision making.

She is a Liveryman of the City of London, a Fellow of the BCS, a Member of the IEEE, a past Member of the Computing Science Committee of the UK's Science Research Council and a Council Member of the Economic and Social Research Council, an ICL Fellow Emeritus, and author of *Scenario Planning – Managing for the Future*, also published by John Wiley & Sons, Ltd. She is a Fellow of St Andrews Management Institute and can be contacted on gill.ringland@btinternet.com.

Acknowledgements

As the century turned and the pace of life grew ever more frenetic, the question was asked: Is there a need for "The Art of the Short View"? – referring to Peter Schwartz's *The Art of the Long View* (Schwartz, 1997). This book brings together thinking about the future and recognizing models of the world, and ways of making better decisions in business in the short as well as the long term.

It is the result of many conversations and shared experiences with people concerned to improve business effectiveness. It tries to address the questions most frequently asked, as well as those that should be asked, by people concerned to discover whether they should use scenarios in their organizations, as well as those wanting to use them more effectively.

It is the product of a virtual team of thinkers and practitioners: Frans Berkhout, Clem Bezold, Adrian Blumfield, George Burt, Napier Collyns, Adrian Davies, Ged Davis, Chris Ertel, Alexander Fink, Maureen Gardiner, Philip Hadridge, Barbara Heinzen, Julia Hertin, Glen Hiemstra, Tony Hodgson, Annette Hutchinson, Eamonn Kelly, Jaap Leemhuis, Tom Ling, Peter McKiernan, Nancy Murphy, Richard O'Brien, Jay Ogilvy, Drew Overpeck, John Reynolds, Sue Roberts, Jan Rotmans, Gareth Price, Kent Potter, Peter Schwartz, Adam Scott, Oliver Sparrow, Jonathan Star, Rohit Talwar, Philip van Notten, George Vervuurt and many others. To all, my sincere thanks for their ideas, their thinking and their vision; and to those, in addition, who contributed sections or case studies, my debt is clearly visible and acknowledged with their contributions.

Additionally, my thanks are due to Napier Collyns and Sue Roberts for reading the manuscript and providing suggestions that have immeasurably improved the book.

And, not least, my heartfelt thanks to Gordon Ringland who added insight at points where it was needed, and to Diane Taylor of John Wiley who published the first "Scenario Planning" book and encouraged this and its sister book to follow it up.

Parts of this book are based on case studies or discussion from *Scenario Planning – Managing for the Future* and these are reproduced by permission of John Wiley & Sons, Ltd.

Abbreviations

AFA	Alternative Futures Associates
BCS	British Computer Society
B2B	Business-to-Business
CAF	Consider All Factors
CHP	Certified Health Planners
D2D	Design-to-Distribution
Dx	Diagnostics
EC	European Commission
ECD	Energy Conversion Devices
EDI	Electronic Data Interchange
EU	European Union
FM	Facility Management
GBN	Global Business Network
GIC	Global Integrated Communicator
Gx	Genetics
IAF	Institute of Alternative Futures
ICL	ICL, formerly International Computers Ltd
ICT	Information and Communications Technology
IDON	IDON Group, now known as Metabridge
IEEE	Institute of Electrical and Electronic Engineers
IPCC	Intergovernmental Panel on Climate Change
IT	Information Technology
KF	Key influence factors
LAN	Local Area Network
NCR	National Cash Register, a computer company
NUD*IST	A software package
OECD	Organization for Economic Corporation and Development

OPEC   Organization of Petroleum Exporting Countries
PEST   Politics, economics, society, technical
PIMS   Profit Impact of Market Strategy
Rx   Therapeutics
ScMI   Scenario Management International AG
SLA   Science Level Agreement
SMG   Strategic Management Group in Texaco
SRI   Stanford Research Institute
SWOT   Strength, Weakness, Opportunities, Threats
TDIP   Therapeutics and Diagnostics Integration Project Team
TESI   Texaco Energy Systems Inc.
WIRED   A magazine
Y2K   Year 2000, used in discussing computer system failures

INTRODUCTION

THE AUDIENCE FOR THIS BOOK

This book focuses on the use of scenarios in business. It is intended for busy, practising managers, managing in unpredictable times. It is also designed to be useful for Management courses because, with the exception of Part 1, sections can be read independently.

The challenge

There has been much discussion at the dawn of the new century about the challenges faced by society. Despite dazzling techno-logical progress, many of our social structures have not matched the pace of change. For example, biotechnology and information technology issues remain poorly integrated into our ethical, social or legal framework.

The new global politics, driven by instant TV coverage and the empowerment of people, focuses on wants rather than needs and is different from the world known for much of the last century. Also, concerns grow about our ability to maintain our physical environment.

The world is more complex than that envisaged when many of our institutions were created, and the institutions are now creaking, facing significant new challenges and pressures. It is tough to be a manager in a time of such uncertainty. Decisions taken today will have effects years hence, but in what sort of world?

Futurists differ on the extent and nature of differences and similarities between today and the future. This situation is further complicated by confusion about the present and the fact that, more than ever, "today" is far from static: it is harder than ever to discern current trends and realities. At a time when the pace of change requires managers to make decisions at more junior levels than before, it is increasingly difficult to make well-informed decisions. There are no silver bullets.

What are scenarios?

The word "scenario" is used in many ways. Military scenarios are detailed contingency plans for a wide range of eventualities; in the creative media, it may mean a storyline; financial controllers use the term to mean sensitivity analysis; and strategists, policy makers and planners use scenarios in a "future-oriented" sense. And it is this that is the focus of this book.

Michael Porter defined scenarios as used in strategy (Porter, 1985) as:

> ... *An internally consistent view of what the future might turn out to be – not a forecast, but one possible future outcome.*

Scenarios are possible views of the world, providing a context in which managers can make decisions. By seeing a range of possible worlds, decisions will be better informed, and a strategy based on this knowledge and insight will be more likely to succeed. Scenarios may not predict the future, but they do illuminate the drivers of change: understanding them can only help managers to take greater control of their situation.

The case studies described in this book include the use of scenarios in connection with political and economic uncertainty, changes in industry structure, new markets, new business opportunities, customer strategy, skill requirements and business disposals. Additionally, scenario thinking is increasingly being used as a way of creating a shared view among a management team. Scenario thinking, by setting discussions in a time frame beyond their current assignment and beyond facts and forecasts, allows for a discussion with less defensive behaviour and a more shared sense of purpose.

2

Scenarios and management toolkits

Managers already have access to a number of strategic management toolkits that can improve the quality of decisions. Most managers will be familiar with techniques such as SWOT (Strength, Weakness, Opportunity, Threat) analyses, Market Attractiveness/ Core Competence matrices for testing portfolios, business value analyses and others. This book provides the background and case studies to allow managers to place scenarios alongside these tools.

There is an important distinction between scenarios and traditional techniques. Scenarios are tools for examining possible futures. This gives them a clear and distinctive role compared with standard toolkits or techniques that may be based on a view of the past. Furthermore, by combining scenarios with traditional techniques (e.g. SWOT for scenarios in 10 years' time), possible futures can be compared. In a changing and largely unpredictable business environment, assessing possible futures for your organization is one of the best ways to promote responsiveness, flexibility and preparedness, often the source of significant competitive advantage. Understanding and preparing for the future is certainly possible through scenario planning.

This book is designed for managers who recognize the complexities of managing in a world where the only constant is change and, increasingly, the only certainty is uncertainty.

The benefits of the scenario approach

Scenarios have been in use at Royal Dutch Shell since the 1960s, largely driven by one of the founders of modern scenario thinking in business, Pierre Wack. The main benefits of scenarios are outlined by Shell:*

Scenarios help us to understand today better by imagining tomorrow, increasing the breadth of vision and enabling us to spot change earlier.

---

*For further information, see "Scenarios – An Introduction", on www.shell.com

3

Effective future thinking brings a reduction in the level of "crisis management" and improves management capability, particularly change management.

Scenarios provide an effective mechanism for assessing existing strategies and plans, and developing and assessing options.

Royal Dutch Shell also point out the benefits of participating in a scenario-building process:

Participating in the scenario-building process improves a management team's ability to manage uncertainty and risk. Risky decisions become more transparent and key threats and opportunities are identified.

The participatory and creative process sensitizes managers to the outside world. It helps individuals and teams learn to recognize the uncertainties in their operating environments, so that they can question their everyday assumptions, adjust their mental maps and truly think "outside the box" in a cohesive fashion.

How this book is organized

This book is divided into four parts. *Part I* outlines the experience of using scenarios in a typical company. The intention is to introduce many of the concepts "in action" for a reader new to scenarios.

Part II describes the framework and environment for specific scenario projects and for scenario thinking. It describes where we are now, the organizations using scenario planning and in what circumstances. It also discusses shortfalls with forecasts and explores the trends that will influence the next 20 years.

Part III is concerned with "making scenarios work" and provides a collection of action-oriented checklists. They aim to act as a reminder rather than a first introduction and are based on personal experience.

Part IV contains case studies illustrating the scope and value of scenarios. As acknowledged individually, the managers or team leaders responsible for each scenario have provided their insights and the views expressed are their own. The final section of Part IV summarizes the conclusions from the book about the role of scenarios in strategic management.

In this introduction and again in Part II, some paragraphs are printed in bold italic: these are sections which are particularly useful for those trying to grasp the reasons for the successes of scenarios thinking in those organizations that have used them.

There is a parallel book to this one that focuses on the use of scenarios in the public sector, *Scenarios in Public Policy*. Here, two themes emerge: emphasizing the similarity of scenarios in the public sector to those used in business. The first theme is the exploration of changes in the external environment, and the second creates a shared vision among stakeholders – voters and citizens – with the aim of steering future developments. Both themes have strong echoes in the direction scenario thinking is taking in the private sector.

How scenario thinking is changing

This book builds on *Scenario Planning – Managing for the Future*, which was published in 1997. That book reflected what I found out as I used scenarios as a practising manager up to 1996, and contained much source material on methodologies, scenarios and case studies.

Some things have not changed since then: venture capitalists still bemoan the "one world" vision of business plans, major corporations are taken by surprise by changes in customer behaviour, new opportunities and new competition. But since 1997, scenario thinking has moved further into the business mainstream for strategy and planning. And scenarios are increasingly being used as tools for knowledge management of complex worlds and as management development tools.

The applications of scenarios have changed their emphasis: in 1997, scenarios were often aligned with corporate planning and portfolio management. Now, scenarios are increasingly concerned with getting the big picture right. For instance, many industries are facing drastic change because of the introduction of information technology, as illustrated in the case studies on the paper and new car distribution industries. Others look to scenarios to create a common language and vision, as highlighted in the case studies on the pharmaceutical and oil industries.

This book reflects the world of the new century – the new environment for strategy and for scenarios – and tries to anticipate those further changes yet to come.

PART I

EVOLUTION IN THE USE OF SCENARIOS

SUMMARY

This part introduces the vocabulary and thinking of scenarios in the context of an average company's (ICL) experience of using scenarios as part of planning, extending into corporate learning, tracing the evolution in the use of scenarios from pilot projects at HQ to adoption into the strategic development of the company, over six years. The use of scenarios was divided into three main projects.

In the first project, scenarios were part of Vision 2000, a project to envisage the IT industry in the year 2000. The scenarios focused on economic growth and technology adoption as the main uncertainties. But what was found was that the team had not been imaginative enough, and that meeting the changes in industry structure and competition dominated the outlook for the medium term.

The second project was based around the question: "What is the added value that customers get from ICL?" The question was very real to the front-line staff, who were used to shipping computers but unsure how to value services. This project created a set of scenarios that were widely used in corporate planning and by a wide range of management teams. The scenarios also led to the adoption of a series of initiatives with the EC and governments to explore the emergence of the Information Society.

The third project was based on adopting and extending existing scenarios rather than creating scenarios from scratch. Its use was to explore the economic futures and trading blocks possible, in order to develop a strategy for global vs. local (e.g. national scale) customers.

Vision 2000

ICL first began experimenting with scenario planning in 1993. It was part of a comprehensive examination of the forces acting on the information technology (IT) industry and a re-examination of ICL's vision of the future. The project Vision 2000 exposed a number of major underlying trends in the industry, which were used to restructure the company.

ICL'S FUTURE

Like many other companies in the IT industry, ICL had been growing within an industry with double-digit growth most years for more than a decade. But the growth masked major changes in the industry. In 1986, we had correctly foreseen that the industry was moving towards personal computers and systems integration. What we had not foreseen was the extent to which the industry would restructure and new players dominate niches, and how far margins would decrease as the industry restructured. So we decided that we needed to take a systematic look ahead to see what opportunities and potential dangers were lying in wait.

We set up a project called Vision 2000 to investigate forces in the industry and the ways in which we could meet the changing needs of our customers.

There were three strands to Vision 2000.

1. External trends
One was looking at the outside world, the conventional PEST (politics, economics, society, technical) factors. It was a question

of gathering statistics and information, concentrating on the mega-trends – such as what was happening in the USA as opposed to Asia and what is happening to demographics – to get a feeling and a reach for the wider environment.

2. The IT industry

The second strand was analysing the IT industry, looking for discontinuities in sectors such as consumer electronics and telecommunications, examining the competition, and listening to who was saying what about future business directions. We sensed that what had been a monolithic computer business was splitting up, so we turned to the PIMS database (Buzzell, 1987) to look for other industrial parallels for the diverging parts of the IT industry. We used the construction industry as a comparison with those parts of our business that dealt with large projects; we looked at utilities for their resemblance to the services business, and consumer electronics for the products/technology-based business. In each case, we charted the distribution of competitors, operating profits, the return on investment, investment required and the management profiles.

3. ICL's assets

The third strand was to understand ICL's assets: we decided on a SWOT analysis of ICL's assets, business by business. We were able to separate ICL corporate assets from those unique to a particular business (e.g. the infrastructure across Europe vs. applications software for in-store retail systems).

THE SCENARIO-PLANNING PROJECT

At the same time as we were pushing ahead on Vision 2000, we were experimenting with scenario planning to judge how effective an approach it could be in helping the company inform decisions.

The scenario-planning group met about once a week over 10 weeks. The meetings were held in the office and consisted mainly of brainstorming. From those meetings, we developed three scenarios, with each one set in the context of a number of basic driving forces: general geo-economic/political conditions, world GDP growth, monetary system/Europe, price stability (especially energy), armed conflicts (defence spending), telecommunications harmonization and what might happen as a result of integration or otherwise of Europe.

We found that there were trends common to each of the scenarios, which dominated the outlook.

TRENDS COMMON TO ALL THREE SCENARIOS

Trends covering economics, technology and the information industry were common to all three scenarios and formed part of our input to Vision 2000.

Shifts in economic power
GDP growth and growth per capita would be lower in Europe than the other two major blocks (North America and Asia).

Population growth in South-East Asia, China and India was expected to cause an increase in the buying population and its capacity to spend. This was in contrast to the forecast of no or low population growth in the USA/Japan/Europe, when disregarding the effect of immigration.

The increasing cost of caring for the old would be balanced by the decreasing cost of educating the young in the USA/Japan/ Europe in the timescale considered, though the swing in the nature of the expenditure would cause social disruptions.

Having a more direct effect on the IT industry, the other shift in economic power that we projected was reduction and change in the role of IT departments. We foresaw purchase of IT would be considered by the Board for large systems integration and facility management (FM) (i.e. for large expenditure), by user departments for applications solutions and line-of-business needs, and by end-users for PCs and shrink-wrapped software packages.

Technology push
The single most important factor affecting the industry in 1993 was the continuing applicability of Moore's law. This law says that the processing power on a chip doubles every 18 months as a result of

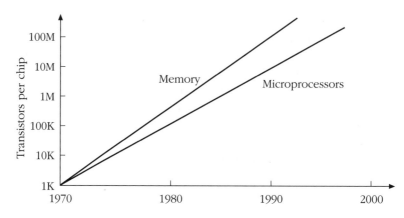

Figure I.1.1 Moore's law (reproduced by permission of Intel).

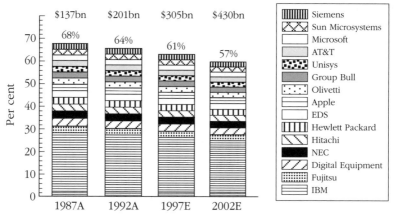

Figure I.1.2 Revenue-based market share of 1992's top IT suppliers, worldwide (reproduced by permission of Gartner Group).

competitive forces, adoption of new technology and new fabrication plants. Moore's law has held good up to the present time (2002) (Figure I.1.1).

IT industry

Based on the view of the Gartner Group (Figure I.1.2), we assumed the IT industry would continue to grow. Gartner estimated that by

2002, 57 per cent of the industry sales – then worth US$430 billion – would be dominated by the major players, although IBM's share would be less than in 1992. Growth would be accompanied by more fragmentation, with more companies entering the market.

Finally, and perhaps more significantly, it was becoming clear that the boundaries between once distinct sectors of the information industry would increasingly shift, with computers and telecommunications moving closer together. The same trend applied to computers and entertainment, media and publishing, distribution, education, consumer electronics and office equipment.

THE SCENARIOS

We called the three scenarios *Stagnation, Baseline* and *Technogrowth*. They differed in rate of economic growth and technology adoption. We used a framework for analysing technology-based industries developed by SRI International to describe the scenarios, after failing to communicate with a table-based approach. The axes of the framework are consumer needs/demands, business needs/demands, and the macroenvironment and delivery structures.

When we rated each of the three scenarios in terms of the rate of change (very high, high, medium, low) on these axes we arrived at Figure I.1.3. This approach helped to begin to tease out the significant differences between the scenarios. They had acquired a different characteristic footprint and could no longer be thought of as "high/baseline/low".

The *Technogrowth* scenario showed a high or very high rate of change in consumer and business demands, but only medium economic growth in Europe.

The *Baseline* scenario was very low in terms of changing delivery structures; it had medium growth of consumer needs/demands, static or declining business needs/demands and a less healthy macroenvironment in terms of growth.

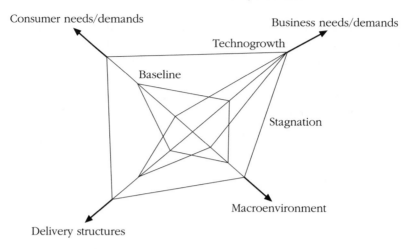

Figure I.1.3 Three scenarios (Ringland, 1997; reproduced by permission of John Wiley & Sons, Ltd: source: ICL).

In the *Stagnation* scenario, business needs/demands would be very high, but they would be about reducing costs with particular demand for outsourcing. Consumer demand would be very flat, with a low-growth macroenvironment and delivery structures would be relatively stable.

Using these scenarios allowed us to make mental jumps, to examine how different elements are connected and to predict that some areas would be more resilient than others. For example, we could see that outsourcing could be viable when the economy booms because people had discretion to rethink their business, and it could be viable when the economy was bad because people were trying to get efficiencies. So, different forces would drive outsourcing in different scenarios. That was a useful perception as we developed our outsourcing business.

The format highlighted the differences between the scenarios and helped us in discussing them with management teams. But they did not "live", and it proved difficult to incorporate the scenarios into planning.

However, on the whole, we were happy with what we had learned from the pilot.

LESSONS LEARNED

With hindsight, we saw a number of reasons that made us less successful than we would have liked:

- We had not started with a specific question that we were trying to answer. You need a question to answer to put the scenario into context and to differentiate the scenarios: our main differentiators of growth and technology adoption "emerged".

- Presentation was initially very unhelpful. The scenarios were spread over three pages in very small type, with far too much detail and lacking any representation of the essence of the scenario.

- The scenarios representation (Figure I.1.3) using the axes suggested by SRI (consumer needs/demands, business needs/demands, delivery structures and macroenvironment) made us also realize the importance of using graphical techniques. It allowed us to home in on delivery structures as an area of major change, and to see that demands on IT would be severe in both the Technogrowth and Stagnation scenarios. However, we found that it required a very detailed commentary and re-conciliation of the axes to use for exposition.

- We did not have a planning framework in which to place the results. There was little way anyone who had not been through the exercise could get a feeling for what we had understood or the implications.

- Having three scenarios proved to be dangerous, particularly in an industry where it can be assumed that people are reasonably numerate and literate. They will usually make what seems to be the sensible assumption that the middle one is the forecast, which limits the value of scenario thinking.

- The very strong trends of shift in the balance of power away from IT departments, of technology push and of growth in the IT industry swamped the differences between the scenarios.

15

- We held the sessions in the office and probably did not think as laterally as we should have.

OUTCOME OF VISION 2000

Overall, Vision 2000 proved its worth in helping ICL to draw up a coherent picture of where the industry was moving. In January 1994, the company was reorganized into three main business streams: systems integration for project-based business, a services-based business specializing in outsourcing and the technology/product divisions. Although we had experimented with scenario planning, it was other tools such as competitive benchmarking and the SWOT analysis that laid the foundation for the changes in 1993. We integrated the trends analysis but not the variable part of the scenarios into the other strands of Vision 2000.

A scenario project to reorient ICL's portfolio

Scenarios are a way of identifying the big questions and possible answers about the future. But how to get started? Who should do the project? How long will it take? How many scenarios? The next five sections describe a project on scenarios for Information Markets that underpinned a number of decisions over several years.

BACKGROUND

ICL was facing worry among its staff about the ability of the organization to meet the needs of new markets. What were these new markets and how could ICL address them? So, the author was asked to provide a framework for analysing the ICL portfolio and for orienting it towards the areas in which our customers would be looking for help. One audience was the Managing Directors and headquarters staff concerned with strategic planning. However, we decided that we also wanted the output to be accessible to managers who make day-to-day decisions; in ICL, they managed units of 30–100 people. We decided that creating concrete alternative pictures of possible futures (i.e. scenarios) would help staff to see how to be successful in different worlds.

We also had to define the scope of the scenarios. Should we consider global economic scenarios or the IT industry? What would dominate ICL's ability to succeed? And how far ahead did the project need to look – five years, ten, more? We decided to concentrate around the IT and converging industries and to take a 10-year view.

SCENARIOS FOR INFORMATION MARKETS IN 2005

Why Information Markets?

It had become clear to us that an information industry was being formed from the computer, telecom, education and entertainment industries. We felt that the impact of this would revolutionize our markets over the next decade, in the same way as microprocessors had revolutionized the computer and electronic industries over the previous decade.

Why 2005?

ICL's corporate planning period, the timescale over which the individual businesses plan, was three years. The planning at HQ extended over five years. What we wanted to do was to take a timescale that was long enough to prevent us extrapolating forward, long enough to force a fresh look, but was not beyond imagination. In addition, to change the culture of a company of ICL's size takes 10 years. So, we voted for 2005.

METHODOLOGY

In planning our methodology, the best overall guide to process that we found was the checklist in Peter Schwartz's *The Art of the Long View* (1997) (see Part III).

Gathering input on the issues

To identify the focal issue or decision, we carried out a round of interviews with some 50 senior staff, both old-timers and those new to ICL. Some interviews were carried out over the phone, others were face to face. They normally lasted half an hour: though some interviewees got interested and discussed a range of ideas for several hours, while others lasted only 20 minutes.

The interviews had two objectives: to get management buy-in for the project and to understand or elicit the burning question for the organization.

In other words, sitting at their desks in 2005, what would the management have liked to have known about in terms of political, economic, societal, environmental, technological and lifestyle trends 10 years earlier? What was the "if only we had known that …" fact?

To unlock the answers, a set of seven questions was used, as suggested at a training session on scenario planning run by the Strategic Planning Society, based on those used by Shell.

Seven questions for the future

Most people have an understanding of how their world works, but often it is not voiced or shared. This questioning technique (Table I.2.1) works on the basis that people know a great deal, but do not always know what they know.

These questions are to trigger thinking: the key is to understand the person's perceptions and unlock their strategic thinking. The technique could be used on an organization, a company, an industry or even a country. It should be done for a specific area of interest and over a relevant timescale.

In Table I.2.1, we amended question 7 slightly to ask:

Imagine you are currently in 2005 and looking back on 1995:

a. What three things would you like to know?

b. What would you like to have done if all the constraints had been removed?

We also added a question:

How do you see ICL in the future?

The reason for adding the ICL question was that many of the topics raised in pilot interviews concerned internal issues. Having an understanding of the person's view as to the type of company ICL would be in 10 years' time made analysing the internal issues easier.

Table I.2.1 The vital issues (the oracle) (Ringland, 1997; reproduced by permission of John Wiley & Sons, Ltd; source: ICL)

1. *Critical issues* Would you identify what you see as the critical issues for the future? When the conversation slows, continue with the comment: Suppose I had full foreknowledge of the outcome as a genuine clairvoyant, what else would you wish to know?

2. *A favourable outcome* If things went well, being optimistic but realistic, talk about what you would see as a desirable outcome.

3. *An unfavourable outcome* Conversely, if things went wrong, what factors would you worry about?

4. *Where culture will need to change* Looking at internal systems, how might they need to be changed to help bring about the desired outcome?

5. *Lessons from past successes and failures* Looking back, what would you identify as the significant events which have produced the current situation?

6. *Decisions that have to be faced* Looking forward, what would you see as the priority actions that should be carried out soon?

7. *If you were responsible (the "Epitaph" question)* If all constraints were removed and you could direct what is done, what more would you wish to include?

THE CENTRAL QUESTION

During the interview process, many interviewees referred to external trends that were worrying them (e.g. related to trends away from mainframe computers). They also brought up areas where staff were uncertain (e.g. the changes in buying habits of our customers, new competitors and markets). Although the team could have created the list from a search of the literature, by asking ICL senior management we were able to ensure they had covered what they considered as the key uncertainties for ICL. The resultant scenarios would then be relevant and challenging but not "shocking" enough to get in the way of their use.

We reviewed the interview scripts and created a list of 60 factors. When we analysed them, we found that one-third of the interviewees explicitly raised, as a critical concern, what will be ICL's source of added value? And the question was implicit in the answers of another third of the interviewees.

We thus decided that, in terms of the scenarios, we should focus on the question:

What added value will we provide to our customers in 2005?

We added the hypothesis that one source of added value would be working with our customers to "innovate to improve their business". The "opposite" to this would be to "minimize their risk".

THE TEAM

In some environments, it might be more suitable for a senior management team, or management team of a business unit, to engage in the process. What we decided was best to meet our aims was to pull a group of staff into HQ who could work with the businesses to explain and exploit the scenarios once they had been created, if necessary modify or extend them, and explore the implications.

We wanted the group to encompass diversity but also be reasonably empathetic to the concerns of the company, so that the company's assumptions were central to the scenario-building exercise. We decided to take the risk that having mainly ICL people might mean that important issues remained unidentified because of cultural blindness, since we wanted to explore the process, the methods and, crucially, how to use the scenarios with the two audiences – the HQ staff and line managers. The group consisted of:

- Paul Clayton: a business analyst who had done research into outsourcing and the changes in the computer services industry, with a MBA from Cranfield Institute of Technology.

- Laurent Douillet: a stockbroker and financial analyst from France who was on a mid-term break from an MBA at The Wharton School.

- Jane Dowsett: an economist by background with specialist experience in market research.

- Steve Parker: a business analyst with specialist expertise in the computer and telecom industries.

- Gill Ringland: Group Executive with specialist expertise in software and the services industry, who led the team.

Steve and Paul had done a short project (SIM 2010) earlier in the year to look at the changes in the telecom industry: this was part of our background database. In fact, networking and changes associated with increased bandwidth and decreased cost had the same central technology-push role in the scenarios project that the decreasing price of processing had in the Vision 2000 work.

HOW MANY SCENARIOS?

We took advice from Shell who had experimented with four, three and two scenarios for strategic planning. What Shell had found was that:

- four scenarios encourage divergent thinking and are useful for creating vision;

- three scenarios lead to the expectation that one is "the forecast";

- two scenarios allowed two very distinct (not necessarily "low" or "bad" vs. "good" or "high") scenarios to be developed.

This approach is very different from the "baseline, high, low"

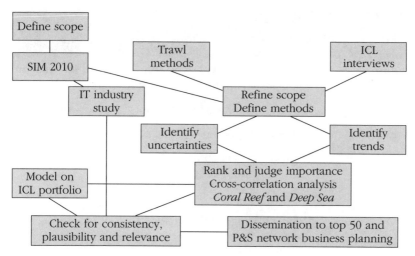

Figure I.2.1 The scenario process (Ringland, 1997; reproduced by permission of John Wiley & Sons, Ltd; source: ICL).

approach, in that it concentrates on creating credible, but different, worlds for each scenario.

TIMESCALE

The main project to build the scenarios ran over three months, with the group meeting twice a week for half a day, as well as carrying out research between meetings. No outside consultants were used, although we did discuss outcomes during the project with friends such as Professor Gareth Price of St Andrews' Institute of Management and Dr Oliver Sparrow of Chatham House.

The scale of the project seems typical of those creating broad-spectrum scenarios, and is qualitatively different from that needed for the workshops used to create common vision and vocabulary, and for team building. And since we were concerned to link to corporate planning, we focused on two "near in", or plausible, scenarios rather than more diverse, or wide-ranging, scenarios.

The process we followed was as shown in Figure I.2.1, and the overall timescale and resourcing is shown in Table I.2.2.

Table I.2.2 Timescale and resourcing (Ringland, 1997; reproduced by permission of John Wiley & Sons, Ltd; source: ICL)	
January	Start of project with work on the "new" information industry – Paul Clayton and Steve Parker
March	Strategic Planning Society course – Jane Dowsett
April	GBN workshop on building scenarios – Jane Dowsett
May	Start data collection – Steve Parker, Laurent Douillet, Gill Ringland, Paul Clayton
June	Start interviews – Jane Dowsett
July	Start building lists of factors, divide into trends and uncertainties – group working, several half-days per week Analyse interviews – Jane Dowsett and Gill Ringland
August	Build correlation matrix – group working, half-days Research on key topics (e.g. electronic cash – Paul Clayton) Define the names and factors in each scenario, build storylines and early indicators – group working, half-days Extract "wild cards"
September	Discuss with other HQ and senior staff, external experts
October	Feed back to interviewees and management team

From data to scenarios

This section discusses the sources of data and the problems of reconciling external sources, interviews, too much and confusing data. Once the significant data are identified, the task is to see the trends and grouping ideas so that the uncertainties are visible. Then the next step is to create a storyline and naming the scenarios, so that they become worlds that live. The difficulties of this creative step for an analytically-oriented team are described.

SOURCES OF EXTERNAL DATA – THE DRIVERS

While the interviews had highlighted a number of factors affecting ICL from the external world, we needed to establish a reference set of data for the project. We found that the main problem was identifying the relevant data from the mass available. In the Vision 2000 project, we had identified good sources for a wide range of IT industry data, telecom research and on technology in general. For economic data, the Economist Intelligence Unit and the OECD provided good background.

The key to relevance is having a mental model of the factors that will be important, and populating the model with values for these.

In our case, we believed that our future would be in a restructured information industry. So data relating to consumer electronics, telecom, publishing, media and professional services were important, in addition to the traditional computer industry.

We also knew that, although the business is global, being based in Europe is different from being based in the USA. So data relating to the development of Europe, and its social model, were key to our scenarios.

Thus, populating the model with data should be straightforward. But, the problem is spotting which factors change radically when a paradigm changes, and which new dimensions or concerns may turn out to dominate a scenario. For instance, when do the changes in behaviour of individuals, as the Information Society takes shape, alter the value chain for our customers? Are there other new developments that could change the rules?

The areas in which we found it difficult to find data were those relating to the wider information industry and to new developments like digital cash. For these consumer-related sectors, we found that often the financial analysts were the best source of both data and opinion at that time.

THE LIST OF RELEVANT FACTORS

We had a list of 60 factors that the interviewees had identified. In addition, we added a number from our researches. We categorized the factors as either trends or uncertainties.

The trends reflected "best educated guesses" about directions. These would be common to all the scenarios. A judgement was taken on which trends were already incorporated in ICL's thinking and processes. For instance, the decreasing role of national governments in Europe and the increasing reliability of hardware were still significant, but perhaps no longer needed spelling out. We were also aware that, even with a well-understood trend, there could be surprises in the pace at which the trends would develop.

"Uncertainties," in the jargon, are "factors over which there are major question marks." For instance, the shape of the consumer market – TV, PCs, broadband, cable was very foggy.

Scenarios are constructed from a number of trends and a number of uncertainties. For instance, while the change in processing power or bandwidth is clearly a trend, the question of whether a consumer market will open up can be treated as an uncertainty: we need to think about the effects if it does or if it does not.

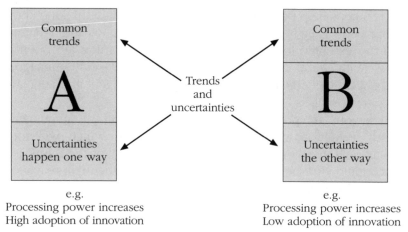

Figure I.3.1 Constructing the scenarios (Ringland, 1997; reproduced by permission of John Wiley & Sons, Ltd; source: ICL).

Figure I.3.1 represents this, using as an example our core uncertainty: Will customers want to take advantage of the technically feasible innovations or will there be a backlash?

GROUPING IDEAS

The process of sorting and grouping the ideas and factors identified by interviews and research is both an art and a science. Scenarios are storylines that combine what we expect about the future with explorations of what may be possible. For them to be useful, the many ideas and factors – over 80 in this project – need to be linked into a relatively few themes for weaving into the storylines. Grouping ideas is an important aspect of building a view of the world that will be of help to the audience in understanding the forces at work and the possible outcomes.

One technique that is widely used has been developed by IDON (Galt, 1997). IDON (now Metabridge) uses coloured, magnetic hexagons, on which topics can be written. The hexagons can then be moved around on a whiteboard until the team are happy with the groupings and can name the themes. This turns out be a very effective way of morphing a shape for the eventual scenarios.

Hexagons help people calibrate the way they are thinking about the present. They help the group to see relationships and dynamics that are essential for understanding the options that are open to them. With attention focused on the whiteboard, on the hexagons and not on individual people, thinking is convergent and language becomes concise.

Hexagons are powerful tools to help develop the language in which institutional learning is embodied and which will form institutional memory. A well-developed memory of the future is a precondition for the company to be proactive rather than reactive – to make its own future rather than submit to it.

THE TRENDS

The trends we had identified were clustered in two areas: those related to demographics and those related to technology. While surprises can occur (e.g. from censuses in the USA, the size and pattern of Catholic immigrant families changed the predicted demographic balance significantly), they are rarer than in the political or social arenas.

Economic/Geographic trends

1. Increasingly sophisticated and demanding customers.

2. Growth in South-East Asia/India/China, with an expanding middle class.

3. Two billion teenagers.

4. Increase in the older population in industrial countries.

5. Continuous restructuring of corporations.

6. Outsourcing of IT is used by half of all Fortune 500 companies.

7. Increasing environmental concerns.

Technology-related trends

1. Bandwidth explosion and development of the Internet.

2. Processing power increases and processing becomes pervasive.

3. Ease of use of technology improves.

4. Digitalization of content and growth of multimedia.

5. Changes in sources of value added in the IT industry.

6. Litigation in IT increases.

7. Semiconductor content of electronics increases.

CORRELATING UNCERTAINTIES

The factors that were seen to be important to us, but with an unpredictable outcome in 10 years' time, were built into a correlation matrix, to see how they related to each other. For example, did one increase, decrease or remain unaffected by another?

The intellectual activity needed to correlate the factors was one of the hardest of the project: we did it with the whole team, in two-hour slots. For each factor, we determined whether it was positively correlated against every other (on a scale of 1 to 3), negatively or not at all (0). Then the factors were sorted, giving the list shown in Figure I.3.2.

We then saw a pattern, in which four themes emerged:

1. The degree of influence/power exerted by governments.

- What will the balance between government-imposed regulation and self-regulation be?

- Will governments regulate to protect national cultures?

- Will government be able to control cross-border information flows and electronic commerce?

2. Social values.

- How important will environmental concerns be?

- Will individual or community values predominate?

- What will the level and forms of security threats be?

3. Consumer behaviour.

- Will there be willingness to take on risks?

- What will the buying points in large organizations be?

- Will consumers become tired of constant change?

- How IT literate will they be or need to be?

4. The shape and degree of global trade.

- What will the degree of intra-block trade or inter-block trade be?

- What will the impact on the West of economic growth in Asia be?

WILD CARDS

Some of the factors were inherently unknowable and not causally linked to any of the others; for instance, the occurrence of a major earthquake in the USA was not caused by any of the other factors, though it could contribute to a factor like "more terrorist actions". The factors that were not linked were called "wild cards". We found that the best way of treating them was to identify where, in the organization, the policy for dealing with them should rest, and to

Shift in technological innovation to SE Asia	5.1	Fragmented industry	−2.9
Loss of government control on info flows	4.3	No terrorism	−1.8
Economic power shift to SE Asia	4.1	No hostilities	−1.1
Greater economies of scale in technology	4.0	Monetary instability	−0.5
Consumer marketing dominates	4.0	Individualism	−0.5
Chance of major breakthrough in technology	3.8	No immigration backlash	1.0
High adoption of innovation (e.g. multimedia)	3.3	No earthquake	1.3
Major IT disasters	3.0	Large professional services organizations	1.7
High economic growth	2.8	EU same	2.7
Bigger and deeper EU	2.7	Low growth	2.8
Boutiques	1.7	No IT disaster	3.0
Major earthquake in USA or Japan	1.3	Low adoption of multimedia	3.3
Immigration backlash	1.0	No major changes in technology	3.8
Move towards community values	0.5	Business-to-business marketing	4.0
Monetary stability	−0.5	Same economies of scale in technology	4.0
Hostilities involving major trading blocks	−1.1	No economic power shift to SE Asia	4.1
More terrorist actions	−1.8	Government keeps control of info	4.3
Full range suppliers strong	−2.9	No technical innovation shift to SE Asia	5.1

Figure I.3.2 Grouping the uncertainties (Ringland, 1997; reproduced by permission of John Wiley & Sons, Ltd; source: ICL).

discuss them, exploring the processes and responsibilities, and getting policies established, rather than building them into the scenarios.

BUILDING A STORYLINE

These groupings helped us to begin to build up the storyline of how the world might look in two different scenarios. We linked open cultures and trading, deregulation/less government, individual values and innovation because of their correlations, and built up scenarios of two different worlds, shown as inner and outer circles in Figure I.3.3.

While having reached a set of themes helped us, it would not have been enough to communicate either to headquarters staff or to management. To provide hooks for engagement, we adopted two illumination aids:

- populating it with a storyline relating to events, geographies, people;

- offering early warning signs or indicators of each scenario.

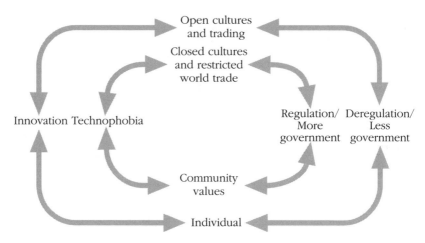

Figure I.3.3 Linking the uncertainties (Ringland, 1997; reproduced by permission of John Wiley & Sons, Ltd; source: ICL).

So, for instance, a pair of alternative answers to uncertainty about the style of marketing – "consumer marketing dominates" vs. "business-to-business marketing" – became in the scenarios:

> ***Consumer style marketing techniques dominate****. Smaller boutique-style companies are successful providing added value as seen by the customer by innovation and marketing. Products and operational services (e.g. help desks, maintenance) are marketed to those who will use them. Individuals will make purchasing decisions for themselves or possibly on behalf of a small group, whether for business or leisure use. This applies for smaller new systems too, driven by cost factors. Only for large infrastructure projects, and complex roll-outs, are business-to-business marketing techniques used. Innovation in products and marketing are mostly introduced by small companies and quickly copied or bought out by the global players. Innovation in marketing and distribution is as important as innovations in technology. Small boutique-style companies specialize – maybe globally – in detailed knowledge of an area, and establish their presence by electronic marketing and word of mouth. Advertising over the network subsidizes payment for content. Outsourcing of information systems is*

booming as many organizations find that managing informa-tion systems is a management distraction. Start-ups using facil-ities in Asia dominate this market through their frontmen in North America.

The "business-to-business" polarity became:

Business-to-business marketing style across the informa-tion industry*. Long-term customer–supplier relationships are cemented by means of framework agreements and loyalty schemes. The big full-range vendors dominate the Fortune 1000 and government, using direct and indirect channels. Out-sourcing is concentrated in these organizations, and profit margins are vanishingly thin, with the full-range vendors taking their profits on hardware and software supply. Smaller companies are served by small value-added resellers who supply hardware and software primarily based on price criteria. Indi-vidual consumers find that vendors regard them as poor relations.*

ALL IN THE NAME

We believe that one reason this project worked better than our Vision 2000 scenarios project was that we came up with names for the scenarios that evoked the essence of what they were about. The names had to act as metaphors so that, when we were talking about a scenario, we could use the name as a short cut to give people an instant and intuitive picture of each scenario, providing a mental framework into which detail could be added.

After much discussion and brainstorming the names emerged – *Coral Reef* and *Deep Sea*.

They seemed to fit well because of the intuitive behaviour that each describes. The *Coral Reef* world is very diverse, with much visible activity and complex food chains. There are many small fish. The *Deep Sea* world is less diverse, with fewer species of mainly larger fish. It is a simpler world in many ways.

33

For people who have land-based reflexes, both the Coral Reef and Deep Sea can be dangerous places unless the reflexes are retrained: for instance, the natural response to danger under the water is to hold your breath and come to the surface. But if you have been breathing from a scuba tank, this is a way to die painlessly with an ascent of even less than 10 feet.

The moral is: training for the new environment is what scenarios are about.

Information markets

This section describes the Coral Reef and Deep Sea scenarios, and their surprising implications for markets that butt up to the core IT industry. The scenarios differ in the attitude of customers to IT, the fragmented or coalesced nature of the IT industry and the extent of regulation: in a Coral Reef world, IT is an exciting and worthwhile investment, and, in a Deep Sea world, customers are looking for suppliers big enough to sue when it goes wrong.

CORAL REEF AND DEEP SEA

Developing storylines for the scenarios took as much effort as correlating the factors: it needed a divergent style of thinking rather than pure analysis. For each of the bullet points, we needed to find examples and exemplars, to think through "how could this happen" and "what would be the milestones on the way". The storylines and early indicators proved to be the second major tool for communication and engagement, after the names of the scenarios (see "Composing a plot for your scenario": Schwartz, 1992).

The full scenarios are described in Ringland (1997). Figure I.4.1 is a summary of the characteristics of the *Coral Reef*, and Figure I.4.2 of the *Deep Sea* world.

Under the *Coral Reef* scenario, the demanding and sophisticated customer expects to exploit the potential for IT to change the business and is interested in new technology.

- Economic background
  - High economic growth
  - Globally interconnected economies
- Competitive environment
  - Highly competitive – survival of the fittest
  - Global specialist players
  - Many local niche players

- Telecoms infrastructure
  - Open, high-bandwidth networks
  - Universal broadband
- Strongest players
  - Highest quality content
  - Best price/performance networks
  - Most convenient devices

Figure I.4.1 *Coral Reef* characteristics (Ringland, 1997; reproduced by permission of John Wiley & Sons, Ltd; source: ICL).

- Economic background
  - Restricted economic growth due to:
    - Protectionist economies
    - Environmental and/or security threats
- Competitive environment
  - Regulation and high barriers to entry
  - Major mergers between content/telecom companies
  - Niche high value segments
  - Local champions

- Telecoms infrastructure
  - Closed networks
  - Broadband only in some major centres of population
- Strongest players
  - Best balance between content/network/access

Figure I.4.2 *Deep Sea* characteristics (Ringland, 1997; reproduced by permission of John Wiley & Sons, Ltd; source: ICL).

Under the *Deep Sea* scenario, the demanding and sophisticated customer is interested in a full-range supplier to take the risk and reduce the cost.

Coral Reef is largely deregulated or self-regulated, while Deep Sea is regulated. *Coral Reef* exploits energy and innovation, with growth from new businesses in new areas. In the *Deep Sea* scenario, Europe and the USA react somewhat negatively to changes.

Another example of the differences between the scenarios is information over networks. In *Coral Reef*, a multiplicity of devices

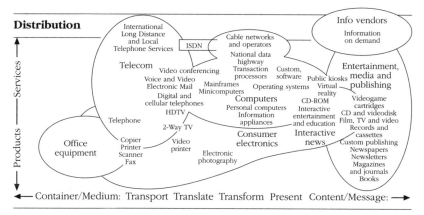

Figure I.4.3 Merger mania: the information industry in 2001 (Ringland, 1997; reproduced by permission of John Wiley & Sons, Ltd; source: Apple).

would connect to a number of competing media supply services, with price wars and confusion/choice. In *Deep Sea*, content would be linked to a conduit, the range of offerings is smaller and through a lower bandwidth – so, less possibility of online movies. The devices would be packaged with the network, and only work with one service provider.

APPLYING TO INFORMATION MARKETS

Before we began to apply what we had learned from the scenarios to the business portfolio, we analysed the sectors of the digital information industry in 2005 (as in Figure I.4.3) in the context of the scenarios.

There were a number of findings, some of which surprised us: for instance, delivery and logistics organizations thrived under the "innovative" and electronic *Coral Reef* scenario and less so under the risk-averse *Deep Sea* scenario:

- *Office equipment* Under *Coral Reef* that market disappears into the computer and consumer electronic markets. Under *Deep Sea* the same happens, but revenues do not decline as quickly.

- *Telecoms* Under *Coral Reef,* voice profitability decreases, with many new entrants and a high growth in non-voice traffic. With *Deep Sea,* voice profitability holds, with few new entrants and lower growth in data traffic.

- *Distribution* Under *Coral Reef,* the number of broadcast channels increase, and mail is largely electronic although parcel mail increases. Revenues grow, whereas under *Deep Sea* they decrease.

- *Marketing and advertising* *Coral Reef* shows high growth in e-commerce in business and consumer sectors, with huge growth in online advertising: US$37 million now to US$2 billion in 2000. In *Deep Sea,* the growth in e-commerce is limited to the business sector.

- *Computer systems and services* *Coral Reef* shows high growth and rate of change, with more companies restructuring, and increase in mobiles and a growth in complex devices. PCs may have different architectures. In *Deep Sea,* there is lower growth and pace of change.

- *Consumer Electronics* *Coral Reef* shows huge growth that is innovation-led. *Deep Sea* has lower growth.

- *Media and publishing* In *Coral Reef,* business use increases, with high growth among the connected, and CD-ROMs and networks both prominent. There is a move to transaction pricing from product pricing. There is lower growth in *Deep Sea,* with home use stabilizing on CD-ROMs.

EARLY INDICATORS

The *Coral Reef* and *Deep Sea* scenarios had differing implications for ICL's strategy. Before basing implementation plans on either scenario, we thought it important to reality-check the scenarios by defining some events that would be seen "real soon" under one or other of the scenarios.

Early indicators of Coral Reef

We thought that early indicators of a world behaving like the *Coral Reef* could include:

- AT&T sells NCR, or Olivetti sells the PC business;

- spin-offs increase relative to mergers in the media business;

- Microsoft constrained by anti-trust legislation;

- information society (e.g. EC initiative) takes off in Europe.

Early indicators of Deep Sea

Early indicators of a world behaving like the *Deep Sea* could include:

- the early indicators of *Coral Reef* are not seen (e.g. the number of mergers increases relative to the number of spin-offs);

- successful lobbying of European governments, to introduce tough new penalties to combat crime;

- IBM centralizes, bringing divisions under central control.

But, of course, neither scenario is a forecast, and neither will happen. There will be elements of both scenarios in the actual outcome, while they may also coexist in different segments and geographies. For example, the USA may be more like *Coral Reef* while Europe may be more *Deep Sea*-like.

We were intrigued to note that within 30 days of each other, AT&T disposed of NCR (*Coral Reef*) and IBM moved to reintegrate its divisions (*Deep Sea*). What this told us was that the telecom business was moving to a different agenda from the computer world, with different economic models and priorities. It led us to concentrate on the telecom sector as customers rather than partners.

The early indicator "information society takes off in Europe" led to a sequence of developments described in Section I.5.

COMMUNICATING THE SCENARIOS

When we had fully developed the scenarios and thought about their implications for ICL, we had to design a communications and decision-making plan. We identified the main groups we needed to reach, and specific Board Members or departments to work with. We gave briefings to a number of groups inside ICL (e.g. the Policy and Strategy Network of corporate planners, the Client Managers and the Board). For this, we used:

- a summary, with an offer to come and talk through the scenarios and their business plan in context of each scenario;

- a slide set;

- a glossy booklet, using images to convey the excitement and dangers of taking a view of the future.

We also included questions relating to dealing with uncertainty in the corporate planning guidelines for the next planning round.

However, we found that working with Board Members on specific problems, such as portfolios of projects for investment, and with management teams on their strategic plans, was the best way to get scenario thinking adopted. With hindsight, we should have identified our target Board Members and specific problems and issues earlier in the project: we could then have involved them in the scenario development process.

Use in corporate planning

Applying the scenarios to portfolio analysis and corporate restructuring, with strategy development, strategy evaluation and risk assessment, helped ICL in its investment and divestment decisions.

The discussion below uses three of the headings by which SRI categorized the use of scenarios in relation to strategy (Ringland, 1997).

1   STRATEGY DEVELOPMENT

Tracking one of our early indicators "*The information society takes off in Europe*" started a train of events. "The Information Society" referred to the EC initiative that ICL had been closely associated with. But the European Parliament had rejected funding. ICL offered to help move public opinion forward through a set of CEO think tanks held with the Commissioner and his staff, and high level attendees from across Europe. This helped ICL also, by clarifying ideas on how the Information Society differs from the industrial society.

Insights
The first insight that we reached was that the levers for change are different in the information and industrial societies. In the industrial society, central government and large companies often initiated change, whereas, in the information society, local government, small companies and individuals take the lead.

In terms of lifestyle, we saw extensive changes in work, leisure, learning, trading, financial services, health care, manufacturing and governance. Following this up with research in a number of forums, what was found is that there are two effects going on. One is that everybody has started to expect to "be treated like the Queen Mum". The second is that the attitudes of people under the age of 30 seem to be radically different from those held by many of the people making decisions – certainly from those characteristic of the over-fifties. The differences covered attitudes to work and the security of employment, and to "community". The increased importance of a sense of community – no longer a geographically-based concept – and the new sources of status based not on price but on scarcity are important to ICL's customers, as they meet the wishes of their customers.

Strategy
The decisions taken as a result of this insight included:

- work on Customer Relationship Management with ICL customers in the retail sector;

- discussions with government on orienting government interfaces towards individuals, by grouping services in relation to "lifestyle events" such as changing a job or getting married, rather than to departmental boundaries;

- development of the Lifestyle brand in financial services, to emphasize the gearing of services to individuals;

- creation of the Lifestyle Network, now incorporated in the Cranfield University New Marketing Research Club.

This example emphasizes that a set of scenarios is a starting point, not an answer. They can provide a framework for deciding to look for certain events or trends, the analysis can prompt more questions, but nothing can substitute for thought followed by action.

2 STRATEGY EVALUATION

This method of connecting scenarios to planning uses scenarios as "test beds" to evaluate the viability of an existing strategy or compare proposed strategies. It is often a good first use of scenarios in a company's strategic-planning system. The strategy may have derived from a set of implicit or default assumptions or a single-point forecast: the approach quickly identifies "bottom-line" issues and provides senior managers with immediate evidence of scenarios' utility.

Applying to a Business Plan

ICL's manufacturing division had been trading as D2D for several years, and increased the amount of work done for organizations outside ICL. D2D's business plans needed to cover a range of external business conditions and customers. We applied the test bed of the *Coral Reef* and *Deep Sea* scenarios to the plans, and realized that the plans were based on a set of default assumptions closely aligned to the *Coral Reef* scenario. When we ran the plans through the wind-tunnel test of the *Deep Sea* scenario, we found that a number of the operational and business characteristics, that D2D had assumed to have very high value, were of less interest to the customers in this scenario. The analysis helped us to decide to sell D2D to Celestica, a global contract manufacturing company.

3 SENSITIVITY/RISK ASSESSMENT

Market Attractiveness/Capability matrix

ICL had used the Market Attractiveness/Capability (MA/C) matrix (Ringland, 1997), as a way of summarizing the portfolio of businesses (Figure I.5.1). The market attractiveness criteria were based on Michael Porter's forces: market growth, barriers to entry, market size, cyclical trading, competitive structure, power of buyers, regulatory position (see Porter, 1985). A ranking of 1 to 7 was used to weight the importance of each. Each criterion was judged to be met well, badly or indifferently by each project, and $+1$, -1 or 0 times the ranking weight were respectively added to the "score" for each

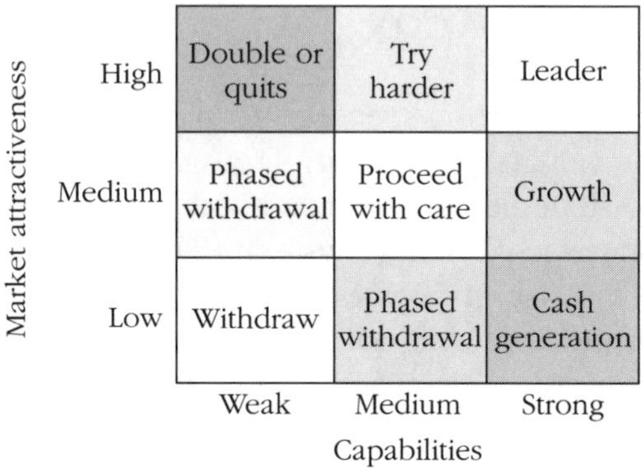

Figure I.5.1 Portfolio management – MA/C matrix (Ringland, 1997; reproduced by permission of John Wiley & Sons, Ltd; source: ICL).

business in the portfolio. So, the best possible project would be scored 28.

The capabilities were different for each business, but the method of deciding criteria, of ranking them and of scoring each business was similar. The businesses were then ranked and displayed on the matrix. Each square suggests a different management strategy.

Investment decision

When ICL was faced with an investment decision – which of seven potential new businesses to invest in – the scenarios helped by providing a different focus for the considerations. For each project or business, the question was what would be the position in 10 years' time under each scenario? Again, a very simple scoring method was used, but it was found that it was necessary to break the scenarios down into about 20 aspects of the description to get a sensible discrimination. Some of these were trends common to both scenarios and others were scenario specific. In Figure I.5.2, the two scenarios are *Coral Reef* and *Deep Sea*.

The change in markets and competencies, and the changing resultant positioning of our businesses on the matrix, allowed ICL to think about the potential new businesses and requirements for new skills, as well as making the investment decisions. Two businesses were chosen from the seven possible candidates. One won the European prize for Information Technology the next year – it

	Social/Economic trends	Technological trends	Deep Sea uncertainties	Coral Reef uncertainties
Market attractiveness				
Market growth				
Barriers to entry	**Is the impact:**			
Competitive structure				
. . .	• **Favourable?**			
Capabilities	• **No impact?**			
Past relationships	• **Unfavourable?**			
Financial				
Skills				
. . .				

Figure I.5.2 Effect of scenarios on MA/C (Ringland, 1997; reproduced by permission of John Wiley & Sons, Ltd; source: ICL).

was in content management – and the other supported BBC Online's growth. They were successful, but, of course, we cannot tell whether the other potential projects might not have been as well.

Analysing the ICL portfolio

We used a staff-training event for a group of senior people to work as a task force to analyse the total ICL portfolio in the light of the two scenarios.

We had previously created a matrix for the portfolio, identifying which units were in market leadership positions ("Business Unit 1" in Figure I.5.3) and which were not, based on our current assumptions about markets and capabilities.

The group at the staff-training event was divided into two teams, one a *Coral Reef* world management team and the other a *Deep Sea* management team. Each was asked to assess the ICL portfolio in 2005 using the same questions about market attractiveness and capabilities, but in the alternative worlds for 2005.

The change in markets and capabilities, and the changing resultant positioning of our businesses on the matrix, were significant (as shown in Figure I.5.3).

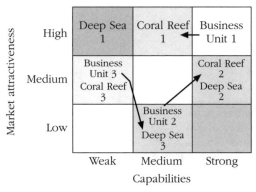

Figure I.5.3 Portfolio of businesses (reproduced by permission of ICL).

So, for instance, the market for Business Unit 1 was attractive, and continued to be so under both scenarios but for different reasons. But ICL's capabilities became inadequate under a *Deep Sea* scenario, while staying moderate under a *Coral Reef* scenario. This meant that unless we could see how to increase ICL's capability (e.g. by moving resources from another unit, by hiring, re-skilling or by acquisition), we should not even consider pursuing this business. In this case, early indicators had a role in deciding whether to "try harder" or to "double or quit".

The market for Business Unit 2 became more attractive in both scenarios, in that it was growing fast. ICL's capabilities were aligned strongly to the market in both a *Deep Sea* scenario and a *Coral Reef* world. The business should be targeted for high growth.

Business Unit 3 did not benefit under either scenario. ICL would stay weak for capability reasons under *Coral Reef* and for market reasons under *Deep Sea*. Under both scenarios, it was earmarked for phased withdrawal (despite it being one of ICL's largest businesses!).

Once the portfolio was visible under each scenario – as above – it was possible to take management decisions about:

- where to invest;

- whether to prefer options that are not highly dependent on the choice of scenario;

46

- whether to compensate for the weaknesses that appear under a scenario;

- whether to concentrate on fast reaction once the likely scenario has emerged.

What we concluded

Our experience of applying scenarios to portfolio management led us to three conclusions.

First, every organization has a culture, based on past successes. This allows people in the organization to make decisions on a day-to-day basis. This is necessary for an organization to function. The problem arises when this culture no longer relates to the outside world accurately, because the environment has changed. It is even more of a problem anticipating changes, which may leave success-ful people in the organization with inappropriate skills or attitudes. For instance, the ICL culture contained a strong belief that the application of digital information was exciting and important. In the early days of computing, purchasers were also enthusiasts. However, the application of digital information is now so per-vasive that our customers – dependent on IT as they are – may, in fact, have a different attitude to digital information. The scenarios work helped us bring these assumptions and attitudes to the surface.

Second, the scenarios we developed had a 10-year planning horizon (compared with our strategic planning horizon of 5 years, with the first 3 in detail). Most people assume that they will be in a different job in 10 years' time. This reduces defensiveness and proprietorial attitudes to specific business possibilities, and allows for a better quality of debate within management teams. The use of alternative future storylines also takes the pressure from intelligent people who know that the future is uncertain. We call this the "unfreezing" effect.

Third, we used the scenarios to move our existing planning tools into a less historic, more future-oriented perspective. Analysis based on comparative benchmarks such as the PIMS database will of necessity use historical data. It is valuable while the operational parameters and business models are stable. We identified likely winners and losers in each scenario, and found that we could imagine major differences in the underlying business model and competitive rankings. For instance, the relationship between market share and profitability in the *Coral Reef* world is very different from that in the *Deep Sea* world, and, as PIMS suggests, vertical integration is the model in the *Deep Sea*, and not in a *Coral Reef* world.

The application of the scenarios to our portfolio using the Market/Attractiveness/Capability matrix gave us a very graphic view of the movement of the ICL portfolio. This is a very simple and dramatic use of planning tools.

4   FLEXING APPROACH

We did not explore the fourth SRI approach, which is to develop a strategy for one scenario and then to flex the strategy against others to introduce hedging strategies, resilience and contingency planning. However, this has been recommended as a good way to introduce management teams to scenario thinking (Mandel and Wilson, 1993), and is fleshed out in Section III.7.

Using scenarios in teams

The scenarios were used extensively with management teams and teams of functional specialists to plan for the future in workshops. This section compares scenarios with brainstorming in terms of productivity, and discusses agendas and timescales for teams and ad hoc *groupings.*

BRAINSTORMING AND SCENARIOS

We experimented with brainstorming and scenarios with the ICL 2020 Group, consisting of people who were in their late twenties or early thirties, so had been with the company for typically about five years, and were nominated as "people who could be running the company in the year 2020".

Brainstorming with this group was found to be counterproductive. It was very difficult to get any sort of coherence of vocabulary and vision, and resulted in people arguing about who was right about the future.

A series of scenario-creation workshops focused their thinking on the potential challenges in 2020. These looked at technology, markets and skills, and directed the group's energies into output that helped ICL to plan for the future.

USING SCENARIOS IN WORKSHOPS

We found that in an organization working in a very competitive environment, with many immediate pressures, it was difficult to get mind share in the businesses for the general concept of scenarios. It was easier for people to understand how to use *Coral Reef* and *Deep Sea*. These scenarios were always greeted with great interest, and discussed very animatedly in any group where they were presented, with every group asking for more detail about their precise part of the business, whether it dealt with local government, law and order, or the market for computers.

Rather than extend the scenarios, we adopted a format that would allow us to work with a business unit: basing the thinking on *Coral Reef* and *Deep Sea*, encouraging discussion and expansion of the scenarios to cover the unit's world in more detail.

We found that a one-day forum could introduce the idea of scenarios, and was sufficient not only to give the team a view of how the scenarios would affect their business plans but also to provide them with a framework for a discussion about their future market strategy. We found that, once the scenarios were presented at a briefing at the beginning of the day, time was needed for the group to identify the additional issues particular to their business in each of their scenarios, in order for them to start adopting the scenarios (Table I.6.1).

To do this, we divided the attendees into two groups, one for each scenario, in order to define extra issues – important for the business in "their" scenario – and for the group as a whole to define additional trends that were specifically important for its business.

After that level of immersion, the group was in a position to talk about the implications from the scenarios for their business.

Skills workshop

Partly as a result of our portfolio analysis, we became conscious of the need to get a clearer view of what sorts of skills would definitely be needed in 2005, and what the skills profile and the personality profile were if the business should turn out to be operating in a *Coral Reef* or a *Deep Sea* scenario.

The format we used for the skills workshop was very much like the one used with the business units on markets. The framework

Table I.6.1 Workshop on markets in 2005

Aim: Develop strategy for Markets in 2005
- Envisage the futures
- Brainstorm the changes
- Plan development programme

Attendees: Functional group (e.g. Distinguished Engineers, Consultancy Managers), management team (e.g. Criminal Justice Department), planning team (e.g. High Performance Systems Division)

Pre-reading: Scenarios for information markets in 2005

Duration: Two half-days or one day

Agenda

First module:
- Briefing on scenarios
- Brainstorm: events & trends specific to the business or function (Syndicates, *Coral Reef* and *Deep Sea*)
- Build list of markets or services for 2005 (Syndicates, *Coral Reef* and *Deep Sea*)
- Report back from syndicates

Second module:
- Assess for each service or market:
  Effect of trends and scenarios
  Size of market
  Key skills, core/bought in
- Report back from syndicates
- Action planning:
  Do now for any scenario
  Watch for early indicators
  What to stop doing

was used in relation to technical skills, consultancy skills and management teams. In most of the workshops, we found that there were one or two people who were absolutely clear at the beginning of the workshop that they knew what the future was, and therefore found the scenarios unacceptable. The best technique for dealing with this was to find confirming evidence for both scenarios in current behaviour, so that people could understand that the future was likely to be as confusing as the present and that it was a question of understanding commonalities and differences and focusing the business on competencies.

There were a number of these workshops. In Project Leonardo, for technical skills, for example, workshops consisted of ICL Fellows and Distinguished Engineers and business unit managers in leading edge businesses. Also included were personnel people and those with responsibility for training. The consultancy work was done with the managers of the various consultancy practices: Figure I.6.1 shows the output from one of the workshops.

SCENARIO WORKSHOP

An example of a scenario workshop, held to establish a common vocabulary as a basis for action, was a two-day workshop organized by the Manufacturing Systems Integration Research Institute of Loughborough University. The aim was to look at the future of manufacturing systems knowledge of the UK in light of global competitive forces. The participants were from the Institute, a range of manufacturing companies in the UK, government officials and ICL, who mostly knew at least one or two of the other participants. The data-gathering stage was low key, and the discussion revolved around knowledge already in the group's heads.

The workshop was oriented toward developing scenarios as a way of unravelling factors that influence the future. It was intended to supplement conventional analysis and forecasting, to provide input to:

• research strategy;

Figure 16.1 Core competencies (Ringland, 1997; reproduced by permission of John Wiley & Sons, Ltd; source: ICL).

Category	Growth required	Delivery	Role	Number
Project management	CR+++ DS+	In-house	B	10-100
Costing metrics and models	CR+++(1) DS+++(1)	In-house	E/G	10-100
Impact of the environment, on politics and economy	CR+ DS+++	In-house/sub	G	10-100
Technology to business transfer	CR+++ DS++	In-house	G/J/E	100+
Change management	CR+ DS+++	In-house	E/J	10-100
Future visioning	CR++ DS+++	In-house	J	10-100
Management services and SLA's	CR+++ DS++	In-house	E	10-100
Systems thinking	CR+++(1) DS+++(1)	In-house	E/G/J	100+
Innovation and information society	CR++(1) DS++(1)	In-house/sub	J/G	10-100
Technical knowledge	CR++ DS+++	In-house/sub	E/G/B	100+
Networking and telecoms	CR+++ DS++	In-house/sub	G/B	100+
Knowledge management	CR++ DS++	In-house/sub	J	10-100
Bid skills	CR++ DS++	In-house	B	<10

Key:
(i) CR = *Coral Reef*, DS = *Deep Sea*
(ii) + or ++ or +++ = Extent of competency growth required for this scenario
(iii) In-house or subcontract = Probable capability strategy
(iv) E = Expert/catalyst role; G = Guru role; B = Body shopping; J = Jester/facilitator role
(v) Number = Likely number of consultants requiring this competency

- business strategy;

- national policy.

It was facilitated and designed by IDON, which also produced the report. The participants commented that the highest value they got from the event was the individual and group insights that were relevant to their research programmes. Their agenda followed a typical pattern (Table I.6.2).

They took 10 years as the time span (i.e. to 2006). Each member of the group started by sharing questions with the Oracle. For instance, one question was: "Worldwide, is the demand for manufactured goods greater or less than current levels?" With these questions in mind, the group saw in the timescale to 2006 a number of things that would stay relatively constant. The group identified these factors as "likely givens".

The group also separated out some trends that were likely to

Table I.6.2   Agenda for a two-day workshop

Day 1

a.m.   Meet, introductions
        Questions for the oracle
        Review process to be followed
        Brainstorm factors

p.m.   Separate the likely givens out from the trends and uncertainties
        Cluster the uncertainties
        Decide on the interesting combinations

Day 2

a.m.   Review the combinations
        Write a scenario story for each chosen combination

p.m.   Describe an evolution sequence for each timeline
        Look for turning points
        Review Oracle questions
        Discuss the implications

affect the future of manufacturing systems. While each of these individually is very visible, the rate of change of each of them can vary and there could be cross-impact. However, the environment for the scenarios is assumed to consist of these "important trends" with the "likely givens" forming a uniform backdrop.

Then, the group concentrated on the factors whose outcome they were even less certain about because of, for example:

- lack of information at the time;

- experts "know" the answer, but experts disagree;

- factors that are too complex or subject to the laws of chaos.

The factors were clustered, and for each cluster a central question was posed that expressed the uncertainty through an answer "yes" or "no". These are referred to as "flip-flops", and those identified by the group are shown in Figure I.6.2.

Out of the eight possible flip-flop combinations, four combinations were chosen which seemed plausible but interesting. They were all different from the group's current forecasts or default scenarios, since the aim was to extend the range of possibilities considered. The central concern was the threat to UK manufacturing from the Far East.

The scenarios would evolve through different routes: for instance, the scenario *All Quiet on the Western Front* was very dependent on high-technology developments and their adoption (Figure I.6.3).

The workshop closed by agreeing on the four scenarios, since there was not time to further reduce the number by reviewing the Oracle questions. The consideration of the implications was left for a later discussion, mostly within the Institute. It was significant that the group had not worked together as a whole before, even though most participants knew one or more of the others. As often happens with new groups, it took a while to develop a common vocabulary: this meant that the progress was slower than might be expected in, say, a management team.

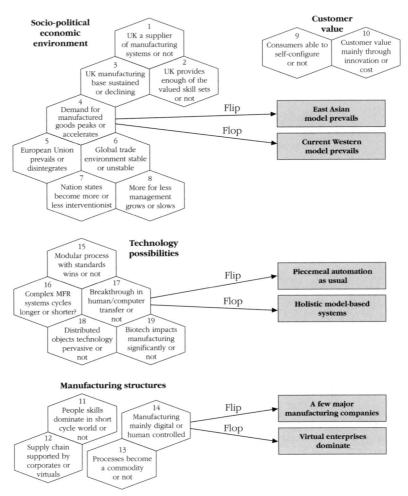

Figure I.6.2 Selected uncertainties for scenario construction (Ringland, 1997: reproduced by permission of John Wiley & Sons, Ltd; source: IDON).

DURATION OF WORKSHOPS

The two-day workshop described is hard work, and it is often difficult to reach the storylines early enough to start thinking about the implications. However, it is possible in two days to develop scenarios from scratch. SRI's Business in the Third

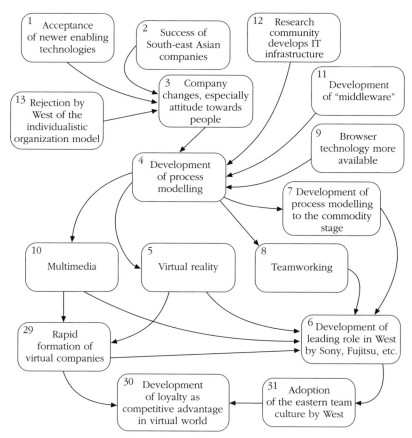

Figure I.6.3 *All Quiet on the Western Front* (Ringland, 1997; reproduced by permission of John Wiley & Sons, Ltd; source: IDON).

Millennium Programme involved sponsors from about 10 organizations, who met three times per year. At one of these two-day
meetings, we developed scenarios for organizations, and were
able to go on to work through the implications for research
(Ringland, 1999b).

ICL have tried out one-day workshops to develop scenarios.
These workshops only seem to be feasible with a relatively
narrow topic area and a group that is used to working together.
For instance, a successful workshop involving the ICL 2020 Group
tackled the topic of "what will be the most disruptive technology up

to 2020", and came up with some useful ideas. The group managed to compress much of the two-day agenda, including thinking about time lines, into one day. On the other hand, a one-day scenario workshop on "work" with a group of participants, who had not developed a common language by working together before, followed the first day agenda of the two-day workshop, and a subgroup was needed to take the combinations away to develop a storyline and recommendations.

Workshops spanning 24 hours (e.g. 4 p.m. to 4 p.m.) provide a way of extending informal time, when participants can develop their ideas offline, and can be successful in developing scenarios.

GBN uses a longer time period – the best part of a week – for the training workshops it organizes, which develop scenarios around one of the participants' area of interest. This provides time to try out techniques such as imagining characters, developing playlets and newspaper headlines of events to enrich the scenarios.

The time difference seems to be important not just for the working hours: allowing relaxation and socialization time for the group, allowing time to rethink and rework ideas, seems to play a considerable role.

Philip Hadridge (Hadridge et al., 2000) has more recently written about working with large, diverse groups using existing scenarios and electronic voting techniques as part of a learning process.

Adopting existing scenarios

The significant factors in the environment for ICL started to be less dependent on industry-related items and to become more rooted in the economic and political forces at work. So, we used externally-developed scenarios concentrating on these factors for strategy development. This section discusses the reasoning behind choosing existing scenarios, their use with two particular groups, and the agenda of workshops to develop strategy based on them.

WHICH SCENARIOS

Three years after the "Information Markets" project, ICL decided that it needed to consider a global perspective as well as the possible shape of the information industry. To do this, it chose to build scenarios on the basis of the three Chatham House Forum scenarios (Chatham House, 1998 or www.chforum.org). There were three reasons for this:

● they were well researched, soundly constructed and provided a macroeconomic framework;

● they had evolved over three years and many iterations;

● they had enough detail to support adoption and tailoring/extension.

The scenarios, which are nominally for 2020, are built around the drivers of the industrialized world. While this may seem to ignore the potential of Russia, China and the tiger economies of Latin America and Asia, it reflects the reality that, together, the industrialized world represents over 80 per cent of the world's GDP, which is not expected to change significantly under any scenario. The four key geographical/ cultural groupings are taken as the USA and its clients, the European group and their dependent sphere, the industrializing nations (or perhaps what is now typified as "emergent markets") and the populous poor nations.

The scenarios are based around two questions or unknowables that will set the agenda if there is not a complete breakdown. The first is the ability of commercial organizations to change: Will they be able to evolve, or break up into smaller organizations or start up new organizations, to meet the environment of continual change? The second is the ability of individuals and society to learn to manage complexity and the new rules, often without role models to help. The ICL scenarios extended the Chatham House Forum work so that they contained more about the IT industry and the main customer groups/industries.

ICL SCENARIOS

One scenario is *Storms*, in which the current chaos turns into a crisis of confidence and depresses world markets for three to five years. Business structures and governments are frozen and there is a crisis of leadership. In the Storms scenario the answer to both questions is broadly "no", change is too hard, and the resulting world retreats into nationalism. In the early years of the 21st century, there are large sums of money washing across national boundaries, put and withdrawn at a hectic pace. This causes a crisis of confidence, and governments in Europe suffer as funds are withdrawn as the competitive position worsens. Unemployment among the unskilled is high, particularly in Europe. Europe and Japan suffer economically and governments "return to their roots", defending national trade barriers. The USA fares better economically and by 2010 is pursuing a free-market model excluding Europe and Japan.

The second scenario is *Market Quickstep*, in which free markets and globalization work to use technology in a way that gives explosive growth to world markets. Business adapts – messily – and governments lose importance. In this scenario, enough organizations and individuals do change to fuel initial explosive growth. This scenario is not inclusive and provides rapidly fluctuating fortunes for organizations and people. The nodes of commerce are "city states" held together by a trading network. Capital is invested for short-term returns and new advances constantly erode value. This scenario is expected to contain periods of growth and correction, with governments providing a reactive environment.

The third scenario is *Third Way*, in which there is well-ordered growth, government and business evolve and find an inclusive route forward, exploiting technology wisely. In this scenario, organizations are capable of change and complexity is managed, but with a difference: business and, subsequently, government attain mechanisms that provide resilient structures based on harnessing knowledge. Governments provide a stable regulatory regime, with agencies providing public services (health, roads, etc.). Rapid economic growth follows, with high returns attracting investment. The industrialized nations jointly implement a regime, through their economic dominance, that aims to change or eliminate "unsatisfactory" governments. This scenario was the ICL "default scenario", which, though unstated, underpinned many management decisions. It determined assumptions about customers and markets, buying decisions and business offerings.

One limitation of the scenarios was that they do not cover two extreme scenarios that are potentially of interest:

- Explosive and sustained growth fuelled by new economic rules, as espoused by many US commentators. However, one scenario, *Market Quickstep*, has strong growth in the short (five-year) term.

- Meltdown of the financial system, with worldwide stock markets retreating to less than half their current value (i.e. the world suffering in much the same way as Japan has done over the past decade). However, one scenario, *Storms*, predicts which, in the short term, markets are in a crisis of confidence and governments are unable to see how best to react.

STRATEGY DEVELOPMENT

The scenarios were used by ICL in two ways: one to advise the European Strategy Board on the range of potential surprises to anticipate, and the other to develop the business offerings strategy with line managers.

European Strategy Board

ICL's European Strategy Board consisted of some members of the ICL Executive Management Committee and a number of non-executives. For this Board, a standard briefing paper approach was used. The Board was not interested in the provenance of the scenarios but was very interested in the short-term implications (e.g. which scenario would anticipate the appreciation of the euro and which its depreciation). For this group, it was important to cover the relative strengths of national vs. regional groupings, and to provide as many early indicators as possible: they were interested in visible outcomes, not causes or underlying forces. They did not like the scenarios that projected the early depreciation of the euro.

Business offerings, customers and competition

We organized two-day workshops for a mixture of high-flyers working in strategy and planning, engineers and marketers, and line managers with responsibility for their section of the annual plan and budgets to match. The engineers and marketers who used the scenarios to think about business offerings became inter-ested in the scenarios themselves. It was important to channel the discussion into "If this scenario happens, what are the implica-tions?" rather than "Can this scenario happen?". We did this by finding current events supporting each of the scenarios and including newspaper clippings as part of the briefing. We could do this because we were using the scenarios as a metaphor – although ostensibly for 2020 – for alternate representations of tensions in Europe in particular.

The timing of the workshops was such that output could be part of the next planning and budget cycle, so that budget could be

Table I.7.1 Workshop to develop business strategy

Day 1

- Brief on trends, focus on IT

- Divide into groups to brainstorm effect of trends on current business offerings

- Brief on scenarios

- Divide into groups to internalize scenarios (e.g. write newspaper front pages)

- Feed back, compare scenarios and fork points and early indicators

Day 2

- Divide into groups to brainstorm effects on current and future business offerings for each scenario

- Develop a time line for significant new offerings each year

- Develop a time line for significant threats to existing or new business offerings each year

- Draft the recommendations and plan how to follow them up

allocated to investigating new markets and customers. The format we used is shown in Table I.7.1.

The group explored the ICL default scenario vs. the two other scenarios and its effect on our choice of target markets and customers. They found that the discussion of how ICL's customer base and competition would vary under each scenario was important in focusing on real differences:

- In the *Storms* scenario, ICL's customers would tend to be smaller, nationally-based organizations, and competition would be national champions. Business offerings would need to be tailored to local standards for user and technical interfaces; local language variants would be obligatory.

- In the *Market Quickstep* scenario, ICL's customers tend to be internationally based, with parent organizations mostly in the USA. Competition would be global. ICL's niche could be in providing local variants for applications – such as government social security – which required it. Alternatively, it could fight on the global front by getting closer to ICL's main shareholder, Fujitsu.

- In the *Third Way* scenario, ICL's main customers would be close to European or UK governments, and the competition would be global. In this scenario, niches are harder to spot and all ICL's traditional markets are subject to competition from a range of other European and US suppliers. The pace of investment would also be slower in the short term in this scenario, due to extensive consultations. This was a surprise conclusion for the workshops, in that the participants had all started by assuming that the *Third Way* scenario was the best option for ICL.

WHAT HAPPENED

Three years later, ICL took the Fujitsu brand to emphasize the ability of the Fujitsu group to service global customers, following the Market Quickstep scenario. At the same time, it separated its business into two, along the lines envisaged in the Vision 2000 project:

- IT utility;

- project management/consultancy.

Lessons learned

This section reviews the lessons learned from the three projects and concludes with a summary of the achievements.

LESSONS LEARNED FROM THE VISION 2000 SCENARIOS

In Section I.1, we reviewed the reasons why we were less successful than we would have liked: missing the big question, content and presentation, lack of a framework for implementation. But the lessons learned informed the planning and application of the Information Markets scenarios project.

LESSONS LEARNED FROM THE INFORMATION MARKETS SCENARIOS

We first used the scenarios we developed, *Coral Reef* and *Deep Sea*, to run in parallel with strategic planning. PIMS analysis of the contract manufacturing business suggested we should divest. The question was: How does D2D look in future markets?

We found that the default scenario of the D2D management team, which had driven their business plans, was near to the scenario in which customers quickly adopted innovation (i.e. *Coral Reef*). Consideration of the structure of their strengths and the market allowed us to reposition the business and proceed to divestment.

We also used the scenarios to evaluate a set of potential new businesses. We had seven "at the starting gate" but we could not invest in them all, so we used the scenarios to evaluate the ability of the potential candidates to operate under either scenario. We chose two and both were successful: one won the European IT Prize.

INTRODUCING THE THINKING

We found that working with the teams responsible for a particular function or market was the only way that we could introduce the thinking into the organization: it is a new way of thinking in an action-driven company. So we learned (again) from Shell and brought out a glossy brochure. We trained ICL consultants to work with customers using our scenarios. And we worked with teams that had specific problems at the time: for instance, using the scenarios to help the consultants and the technical community to plan for a skills portfolio in the future.

We concluded that (as seen in Section I.4), to communicate scenarios in organizations not steeped in scenario thinking, the following are needed:

- a "lift (elevator) speech", which describes the use of the scenarios in relation to a specific concern, or a success story or reference sell;

- clear representation of "the question";

- vivid names and a glossy "storyline" booklet help;

- a good storyline and coherence that people found credible, with memorable incidents on the time line;

- a process by which the scenarios can be used by the organization to decide what to do next.

LESSONS LEARNED FROM ADOPTING
EXTERNAL SCENARIOS

We used the Chatham House scenarios for the industrialized world primarily for a set of focused workshops with managers and designers, etc.

For this, we did not produce a glossy booklet but provided a briefing pack instead, describing the scenarios and containing some additional economic data.

With hindsight, we should have included in the briefing pack additional ICL-specific material, which the managers might have seen before but would have been relevant in the discussion; for example:

- lists of major customers by country and expenditure on IT;

- major lines of business in each of our countries.

Overall, we concluded that it is difficult to know what people do and do not know, so that it is better to be explicit on all counts, whether about the scenarios or company-specific information: it is very easy for a manager in one department not to be aware of major forces at work in other departments.

CONCLUSIONS

The scenarios had the effect of energizing the people involved – in scenario creation or in the workshops – to think about the future in a way that had not been done before in the company. The formulation of scenarios that could be extended – what would this mean for my business or speciality? – allowed large numbers of people to visit the future in safety and to make better decisions as a result.

But the manager shall be nameless who, on hearing that the Information Markets scenarios described 2005, asked if this was five past eight this evening or tomorrow.

PART II
SCENARIO THINKING

SUMMARY

This part provides a framework for understanding and working with scenarios. The intention of this part is to provide a context in which a specific project takes place, to relate scenarios to strategy and to forecasting, in order to improve the resilience and utility of scenario content. Part III follows on and aims to provide the process and practical aspects of scenario thinking.

Section II.1 sketches the development of strategy and strategic planning in business, and the relationship of scenarios to strategy in each. Particularly, it looks at the move of companies away from supplier push into demand pull, and the effect on companies' strategies and use of scenarios. Section II.2 summarizes the four main uses of scenarios: for political and economic uncertainty, for industry restructuring, looking for or evaluating potential new products and markets, and for portfolio management.

Sections II.3 and II.4 are cautionary, suggesting that scenarios may well overreflect the assumptions of their creators, and that these assumptions are likely to be shared by a generation or culture. Even if scenarios pose challenging questions about the future, it may be difficult for organizations to accept their relevance or to act.

Sections II.5 and II.6 provide guidance on factors, and trends arising from technology and demographics, that need to be considered in building scenarios. Section II.5 also suggests that the four pillars of current Western life – work, home, education and government – are likely to be unrecognizable in 20 years time.

Section II.7 summarizes the conclusions of Part II.

Scenarios and strategy

In this section, we discuss the use of scenarios in strategy as organizations change their expectations and methods. As the world changes from supplier-led to demand-led economies, the focus for scenarios has moved from scenarios in planning to scenarios in the storytelling sense. However, underlying this is the role that scenarios have in providing a forum for learning – for individuals, teams and corporations. Many strategists believe that this role is the most significant in the long term. The contributions of Adrian Davies of St Andrews Management Institute are gratefully acknowledged.

MODELS OF THE WORLD

Models of the world are often used to anticipate "real life". For instance:

- Wind tunnels are used to test car shapes for aerodynamic features. Does the car become unstable at high speeds, does it have higher or lower drag factors than other shapes?

- Fatigue tests are used to test the strength of airframes. Either a life-size airframe or a scaled-down airframe is subjected to stresses and strains in a test rig, where early signs of cracks, fractures or breakages can hopefully be encountered before they are seen in the airframes of aircraft flying passengers.

- Mathematical or computer models are used to schedule and allocate resources, within sets of constraints. Linear programming

71

techniques are used to solve problems such as forest management, agricultural production, production planning in factories
and the selection of hospital menus.

It is clear from these examples that, whether physical modelling is
used or whether computer modelling is used, the predictions for
real life are only as good as the ability of the model itself to contain
enough rules and constraints about real life. Two aspects of a
successful model are suggested by these examples:

- the ability to anticipate real-world behaviour – which may be
  unexpected – by exploring the constraints or changes in the
  external environment, or the relationships between forces;

- the creation of a mental model that allows the user to look for
  early confirming or disconfirming evidence.

The question for managers is how to get these aspects into strategic
thinking. It is not easy.

Clausewitz's view on how to act boldly despite the inherent
uncertainties of war was to suggest: "an educated guess and then
gamble that the guess was correct" (for a more detailed analysis,
see Herbig's chapter in Handel's *Clausewitz and Modern Strategy*,
1989). It could be said that scenario planning is a set of processes
for improving the quality of educated guesses, for deciding what
the implications are and when to gamble.

SCENARIOS AND STRATEGY OVER THE DECADES

The use of scenarios in organizations has evolved in line with the
pattern of strategic thinking:

- In the 1970s, corporate planning and complex methodologies
  were driven from the centre, and scenarios were used to
  explore unknown environmental factors or the effect a discontinuous change like the oil price changes;

- In the 1980s, organizations blamed planning for failing to anticipate structural change such as new sources of competition. This
  was an era of supplier-led obsolescence, as markets saturated.
  Mass marketing and the growth of credit changed the attitudes of
  consumers. Distribution was segmented and individualism (or at
  least niched brands) grew apace. In this environment, the
  approach to planning needed to change.

For instance, Michael Porter in his **Competitive Advantage**
*went back to basics and proposed that companies consider
the forces on their markets as a backdrop to planning. He
considered scenarios to be important tools for understanding
and so getting ahead of trends, and recommended the building
of alternate scenarios as a form of sensitivity analysis.*

- In the 1990s, the "Pierre Wack" Intuitive Logics school, as
  practised by SRI and Shell, emerged as the main approach
  (Wack, 1985). The essence of this is to find ways of changing
  mindsets so that managers can anticipate futures and prepare for
  them. The emphasis is on creating a coherent and credible set of
  stories of the future as a "wind tunnel" for testing business plans
  or projects, prompting public debate or increasing coherence.

*As the world changes from supplier-led to demand-led
economies, the focus for scenarios has moved from scenarios
in planning to scenarios in the storytelling sense.*

THE AGE OF INDIVIDUAL POWER

The 1990s saw the full emergence of the age of consumer
power, as product quality was assured and the focus moved to
service. Individualism started to change attitudes towards governments and public services and assumed their roles to be as service
providers. Trust in government and institutions decreased.
Deference decreased and made public sector jobs unattractive.
The power of special interest groups grew and demands grew on
governments.

The need for reskilling of employees and the drive to outsourcing are among the trends that make achieving a work/life balance very hard. Glen Peters's *Beyond the Next Wave* captures a number of these issues (Peters, 1996), and Rolf Jensen's *The Dream Society* (Jensen, 1999) digs under new modes of consumer behaviour.

Much of this change was fuelled by globalization of the media and its scope, and the accelerating rate of technological change. In this world, it is much harder to manage public relations. It makes dealing with routine "unexpected events" such as public safety problems, medical scandals, fraud against the government, education disparities or failures, epidemics or terrorism even more necessary.

These factors are having a destabilizing effect on government, which decreases trust in politicians and civil servants at all levels, creating a business environment with new dimensions.

Table II.1.1 summarizes some of the characteristics of the age of individual power.

Table II.1.1   Changing characteristics of organizations (reproduced by permission of Adrian Davies, St Andrews Management Institute)

From	To
Command and control	Empowerment
Structured life	Unstructured life
Importance of size	Need for speed
Predictability	Uncertainty
Clarity	Ambiguity
Slow change	Rapid change and obsolescence
Reliance on processes	Reliance on people
Hierarchical or managed organizations	Alliances and coalitions
Avoiding risk	Managing risk

SCENARIOS AND STRATEGY IN THE AGE OF INDIVIDUAL POWER

The consensus of the experts is that, in this age, management is easier to talk about than to implement. Competing nostrums include:

- emergent strategy and adjustment to change through feedback (Mintzberg et al., 1998);

- explicit strategy as a rational competitive weapon (Hax and Majluf, 1995);

- balanced scorecards linking strategic objectives and measures to personal incentives (Kaplan and Norton, 2000);

- senior management manages values and implementation at the coal face (O'Reilly and Pfeffer, 2000);

- change and innovation by allowing employees to be entrepreneurs (Hamel, 2000);

- stakeholder model that widens corporate responsibilities;

- virtual organizations that reduce risk for each of the partners;

- passion and vision, vision and leadership (Stopford, 2001);

- etc.

How can scenarios help organizations to be successful in this age? Scenarios are widely used to:

- *explore uncertainty and prioritize issues of potential concern;*

- *pick up weak signals of emerging risks and opportunities;*

- *provide a forum for getting outside the orthodoxy of the organization;*

- *create a common language and the will to implement;*

- *focus attention on external challenges rather than internal issues;*

- *prepare for surprises.*

In addition, authors in strategic management have suggested central roles for scenario thinking; for example:

- Hax proposes that factors identified by means of scenarios be used as part of environmental or business intelligence scans. This is similar to the methods used to track early indicators, but could also be used to develop sensitive probes that anticipate or pick up the start of major trends or changes. An example might be using a McDonalds growth rate vs. the restaurant trade as a whole, to monitor consumer confidence (see Section III.8).

- Hamel and Stopford both believe that organizations should use normative or visionary scenarios rather than business as usual or projective scenarios, to build vision and drive their plans. This approach is followed, for instance, by the Institute for Alternative Futures in their work with the voluntary sector (see www.altfutures.com).

However, underlying all these is the role that scenarios have in providing a forum for learning – for individuals, teams and corporations. Many strategists believe that this role is the most significant in the long term.

Where are we now?

This section identifies ways in which scenario thinking is being used to handle political, economic, social, environmental and technological uncertainties, and to make decisions. Four main challenges have been tackled by scenarios: political and economic uncertainty, industry restructuring, new products and markets, and portfolio management.

WHERE SCENARIOS CONTRIBUTE BEST

This analysis was prompted by a discussion with Jaap Leemhuis of Global Business Network (GBN) Europe. Scenarios are now accepted as a management tool. Where is their use best focused?

- *Scenarios are indicated where the force of the external world requires senior managers to think "outside-in" – as in times of structural change in the industry or its customers.* Examples of this are the change in the energy industry, or the telecom industry, and in government in Europe. Much of the current wave of structural change is the result of the introduction of information technology: in the supply chain, or the customer interface, or by introducing new products. Will the next wave be due to biotechnology?

- *Scenarios provide an environment for creating a shared context.* This is important in many of today's organizations where specialists need to contribute to a shared problem: each will approach it with a wealth of tacit knowledge and comfort in their own domain, or need to defend an existing power base. Examples were discussed in Ringland (1997), which contrasted scenarios with brainstorming as a way of increasing shared comprehension.

● *The use of scenarios to engage the public in policy debate has been markedly successful.*

This is the subject of the parallel book, *Scenarios in Public Policy* (Ringland, 2002), citing examples from the school system in Seattle to Arnhem in Holland.

USES OF SCENARIOS IN STRATEGY

SRI related four different ways in which scenarios could be used in strategy (Ringland, 1997):

● strategy development, the most often discussed use of scenarios;

● strategy evaluation, the use of scenarios as test beds or wind tunnels for existing strategies;

● sensitivity/risk assessment of a project or across a portfolio of businesses or projects;

● testing an existing strategy or plan, or "most probable" scenario against other scenarios to develop hedging or contingency plans.

Examples of the first three were given in Section I.5. Very rarely are scenarios used to rework alternative business plans in complete detail, though one example at British Airways was given in Ringland (1997).

FOUR MAIN APPLICATIONS

Over the past few years, four main issues have been the trigger for much of the scenarios work in the corporate sector. Political uncertainties and cultural issues are often the trigger outside the USA, but were until 11 September 2001 less so in the USA. Industry restructuring is a global issue. Scenarios are also used to look for new products and markets, and to refine business portfolios.

Environmental pressures have stimulated a number of scenario studies, mostly undertaken by governments or NGOs, rather than originating in the corporate sector. These studies, and scenarios to develop public policy in a range of countries, regions and cities, are also described in *Scenarios for Public Policy* (Ringland, 2002).

In the list below, we refer the reader to case studies in Part IV. An asterisk * indicates a case study taken from *Scenario Planning – Managing for the Future* (Ringland, 1997).

Political and economic changes

- The insurance company Erste Allgemeine Versicherung anticipated the fall of the Berlin Wall and made plans to expand in Central Europe.*

- United Distillers (now Diageo) has carried out a number of scenario development exercises to assess the future of markets such as India and South Africa.*

- Statoil (Section IV.2) used scenarios to explore the question "What will be the future patterns of energy consumption?" and, hence, possible strategies for this Norwegian energy company.

Industry restructuring

- In France, scenarios have been used to help plan the way forward for the steel industry.

- The use of scenarios to assist strategic planning in the advertising industry has been described in Schoemaker (1992).

- Caledonian Paper used a joint project with IPC Magazines to develop an understanding of the paper/publishing industries as increasingly impacted by new electronic channels for publishers (Section IV.4).

- A construction company uses the technique for "back of the envelope" examinations of business propositions, and as part of its management of its project portfolio.

- A study of the new car distribution system was used to develop understanding of electronic trading and new car servicing systems (Section IV.3).

- A software product company used scenarios for the restructuring of their industry to drive the development of product strategy for the future (Section IV.5).

New products and markets

- Texaco used scenarios over a period of four years to explore the new environment for oil companies within which investment and policy decisions would be made (Section IV.6).

- Glaxo used scenarios to explore futures for health services in their widest sense, in order to decide their role in those futures, their preferred future and ways of encouraging that future to unfold (Section IV.7).

- Krone is a manufacturer of telecom products such as telephone socket boxes. The company needed to assess the potential impact of optical fibre and the extent to which the use of cable telephones, for example, would affect the existing business and hence to develop new product lines.*

Portfolio management

- A financial services conglomerate used scenarios to help it analyse its portfolio, leading to a break-up of the company into two (Section IV.8).

- Cable & Wireless wanted to find a way of transferring thinking about the market effects of new technologies between the scattered business units in its federal structure.*

- ICL used scenarios to understand the changing market for out-sourcing, to prepare units for disposal, to guide investment in its portfolio of businesses and to develop new strategies in Europe (Part I).

Shell has been very influential in the development of scenarios. The company continues to make their scenarios public: the latest "Energy Needs, Choices and Possibilities – Scenarios to 2050" are on its website www.shell.com. As Ged Davis of Shell says, "by considering future scenarios we aim to make a better decision today or the same decision earlier."

USING SCENARIOS IN THE ORGANIZATION

Scenario planning traditionally used possible future outcomes (scenarios) to improve the quality of decision making (planning), but the emphasis has moved in recent years from building scenarios to successfully using them. The techniques for building scenarios are well developed; the challenge is to incorporate an understanding and facility with possible futures into management thinking. This has led to an emphasis on:

- *Scenario planning used for team development: the process of thinking through alternative futures provides a non-threatening environment for developing an understanding of shared and differing assumptions.*

- *Improving the structural assumptions and data behind planning: "Linking scenarios into the organization" (Section III.8) discusses the role of existing business intelligence activities in the organization in facilitating this, and*

Section II.4 discusses some of the hurdles to overturning historical mindsets and structural assumptions.

- *Techniques for communication of scenarios: when scenarios were mostly used by corporate planners, a table of factors and values would be sufficient to describe a scenario (e.g. the accessible market is 20 million), as scenarios are increasingly used to develop significantly different world views, they are increasingly described through stories intended to capture the imagination (e.g. Allan et al., 2002).*

- *Scenarios as tools for understanding our world today: in many scenario studies, even those ostensibly set in the future, the effect is to help the team recognize patterns of competition or business direction that are relevant in the organization at that time (Oxbrow et al., 2001). Examples include the Trading Group (Section IV.8) and Statoil (Section IV.2) case studies.*

Forecasts

This section discusses systematic cultural issues that affect forecasts of the future. It is included because these systematics also affect the thinking of participants as scenarios are developed. Much of this section is based on "Shocks and paradigm busters" (Ringland et al., 1999a), and is published by permission of Elsevier Science.

DELPHI

The Rand Corporation developed the Delphi technique, named after the ancient Greek oracle, in the 1950s as a method for gathering information about the future. It is based on asking experts in their various fields to estimate individually the probability that certain events will occur in the future. The goal is to get them to converge on future views by comparing their answers with those of other experts (see Amara and Lipinksi, 1983).

It is widely used for technology futures. This is successful because experts have a forward view both of technology in the lab and of the limitations of current technology, which allows them to envisage the roll-out of a new product several years ahead. In Figure II.3.1, technology forecasting is at the "certain" end of the spectrum and scenarios at the "uncertain" end.

Examples of the use of Delphi include the UK's Technology Foresight Programme (DTI, 1996; Georghiou, 1996), the Technology Forecast carried out in Japan for the period 1990 to 2020 (Japanese National Institute for Science and Technology Policy, 1995) and a forecasting exercise by BP to underpin their research

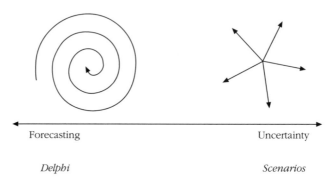

Forecasting   Uncertainty

Delphi   *Scenarios*

Figure II.3.1 Forecasting and uncertainty (Ringland, 1997; reproduced by permission of John Wiley & Sons, Ltd; source: ICL).

programme (Barker and Smith, 1995). However, the survey of the results of the Technology Forecast Programme in Japan has shown mixed fortunes after 25 years. One strong theme was the improved quality of forecasts on a particular topic when a range of experts from neighbouring disciplines were included in the consultation process (e.g. physicists and chemists in biology foresight exercises).

In general, forecasting and trends are very useful in two areas (see, e.g., Section II.5: "Evolutionary models for culture change"):

- Technology developments, where technology in the lab can take a well-trodden track through to the product and the timescale has a quantifiable lower bound (but see the examples of the FAX and microwave oven under "Forecasts of Technological Change" for rates of adoption).

- Demography, where known birth rates and predictable death rates give predictable population sizes, though mobility and biotechnology are causing surprises even here. For instance, between two censuses at 10 year intervals the USA "acquired" 40 million unexpected people. As Ged Davis says: "A trend is a trend until it bends" (Davis, 1998).

On the other hand, social factors dominate the "uncertain" scenario space in Figure 11.3.1.

FORECASTS – SYSTEMATIC ERRORS

As part of calibrating a number of scenario exercises, we needed to understand how possible it is for scenario creators to shake off the tyranny of the present, and what implicit assumptions seemed to be carried into even the most apparently radical scenarios. For instance, scenarios created by corporate employees will reflect their cultural assumptions and they will find it hard to imagine cultures different from their own. One example is the difference in thinking of hierarchical thinkers and the loosely organized networks of NGOs (Davis-Floyd, 1997).

We looked particularly at forecasts related to technology and society to see if any systematics could be found.

TECHNOLOGY AND SOCIETY

Long before scenario planning was heard of, H. G.Wells was visualizing futures based on scientific progress. The predictions of Wells in the 1890s can tell us a great deal about predictions of the future and the environment in which they are made. Wells was a commercially successful author who tailored his publications to meet the preoccupations of his readers in late Victorian England. His predictions were consciously based on gathering the trends and inventions of his present-day society, and extending their development into the future. It is hardly surprising, therefore, that some of his predictions carry in retrospect an uncanny accuracy: Wells lived in a period of rapid innovation and the technology described in his novels (telephones, cars, aeroplanes) had either already been invented or was being discussed.

Other predictions, however, reveal just how contemporary Wells's predictions were. His concerns with class, the conflict between capital and labour, and the merits or dangers of government through an enlightened, rational elite place him firmly in the mindset of late Victorian social commentators and reformers. The genius and limitations of Wells was to grasp the innovations of his time and to realize that they would occupy part of the centre stage of the present. But, while his time machine remained only a device of fiction, he was unable to see the whole.

In general, science fiction and technology forecasting have a better record than forecasts about human behaviour, which remains various and often unpredictable. What has often been underestimated is the capacity of people acting as individuals or in small loose groups, relying on their own common sense. There has also been a tendency to overestimate the capacity of governments to implement.

So, for instance, similar assumptions to Wells's were visible in Herman Kahn and Anthony Weiner's (1967) *The Year 2000: A Framework for Speculation in the Next Thirty Years.* Some of the 100 things they expected to see by the year 2000 included:

- underwater cities;

- the use of the moon to replace street lights;

- the possibility of personal pagers;

- computers in business.

Kahn and Weiner reflected the assumptions of their time in overestimating the potential of governments to implement big projects like underwater cities, and they greatly underestimated the paradigm change arising from technology change based on semiconductors and, hence, business use of computers.

FORECASTS OF TECHNOLOGICAL CHANGE

Steven Schnaars (1989) has studied an orthodoxy that he calls "the myth of rapid technological change". He notes that in the 1960s, for example, tremendous change was forecast for the way transportation would develop, including commercial passenger rockets, VTOL and supersonic planes, automatic vehicle separation on new "smart highways", and the use of nuclear power in all forms of transport.

The people who made these forecasts now seem to have been enthusiasts enamoured of technological wonder. They went wrong because they fell in love with exotic technologies just because they were exotic. It was easy for them to believe what they wanted to believe. They also failed to pay attention to the less romantic matters of commercial fundamentals. Many of the ideas were simply too expensive to be practical. They made some wrong assumptions about human behaviour as well. Consumers might have agreed that they wanted better mass transit systems, but few were happy at the idea of sitting behind a nuclear engine in a computer-controlled bus. On the whole, they did not respond enthusiastically to CB radio or to quadraphonic sound systems. Not all technology is wanted merely because it exists.

Some ideas have come to fruition, but not very quickly:

- The FAX machine is an example of timing. Quick uptake was predicted, but initially it was too expensive and took too long to transmit a document. Eventually, 20 years behind plans, it achieved a mass market through improvements in price and performance.

- It is easy to see, now, that the microwave oven was always a good idea, but it achieved success 25 years later than expected. It was only with changes in lifestyle – women working and improvements in ready and frozen meals to gourmet status – that the ovens proved to fulfil a useful role.

Technologists work within the commonly held assumptions of their time. For example, in the 1960s, when the theme of space travel was popular, many different forecasters predicted manned bases on the moon. In the 1970s, the energy crisis became the dominant theme, and one assumption was that nuclear energy must certainly be the solution.

FOUR SYSTEMATICS

Four sources of common errors in forecasting emerge from these analyses. Checking scenarios or forecasts for sensitivity to these four may help organizations to improve the quality of the assumptions they make about the future.

The individual is unboxed

The first is that planners' assumptions about the behaviour of people, based on previous decades, are certainly not right in the current world. The basic framework of a hierarchy of needs – starting with meeting our basic needs for food, clothing and shelter, and moving on to needs for self-expression and self-actualization – should warn us that people widen the range of choices they make once food and shelter needs are met. And since, today, most people are not prompted by memories of hunger or cold, people's behaviour becomes increasingly difficult to forecast. The common reason for failure of a number of forecasts, particularly the technology-driven ones, was that people were more sensible and capable of choice than the forecasters or planners expected.

This can cause paradigm shifts and shocks to occur overnight, not just the change in correct attitude for the wearing of baseball caps, but in very major ways like the fall of the Berlin Wall.

Government cannot do it

The second is the major political and military paradigm shift, caused by the comparative retreat of governments. Many Western governments are trying to withdraw from the approach they took in the post-war period. Partly, it is because the ability to control their environment decreases as finance moves around the globe more easily, large movements of guest workers and immigrants continue, and technology makes the international transfer of ideas faster and more copious. At the same time, the public's demand for government services constantly increases, not diminishes. While privatization satisfies some expectations by replacing the government in supplying services, demographic and employment pressures reduce governments' abilities to fulfil their post-war roles.

In the bipolar world of the Cold War, the effort by the USA to stay ahead in technology meant that government development funding was large and assured. This resulted in a stream of spin-offs for civilian and commercial exploitation. Now that the Soviet threat has disappeared, funds for research and development have been reduced. The main drivers for technological change must now come from private enterprise. Will the sources and types of technological advancement therefore be harder to forecast? The effect of this paradigm shift is very deep-seated: many forecasts make assumptions that the role of the government will continue to be significant.

Technology will be used if it is useful
The third source of common error is in timescales of adoption of technological innovation. Often, the nature of a development is forecast correctly, but the timing is overoptimistic. A good idea attracts enthusiasts who assume that "normal" consumers will be equally keen. Forecasting the timing of crucial developments requires an understanding of the other components that are needed to form a total system. An important lesson is that a forecast that does not materialize in the expected timescale might not be wrong in its essentials, only in its timescale; so, it should not be discarded too quickly. The other components may come from totally different fields, as in the case of the microwave oven discussed earlier.

This suggests posing the questions: Who would want one of these and what would they use it for? How much would they pay for it? The questions provide a useful counterpoint at a time of hype.

Progress
A fourth paradigm shift is a change in public attitudes. For centuries up to the turn of this century, Western intellectual thought embraced the idea of continual progress towards greater scientific certainty and a more perfect state of being. Ultimately, everything would be explained and all problems would have solutions. The experience of the 20th century has disillusioned many, and preoccupations with worries about issues such as pollution, the nuclear threat, and ethnic conflict have challenged our assumptions about the nature of progress. Now, we do not think that things will necessarily get better. We think we might do well if we can merely sustain things. This loss of optimism is more marked, perhaps, in Europe than in the USA.

Pitfalls and pratfalls

This list has been developed by Dr Barbara Heinzen, based on nearly 15 years of experience with scenario planning, and is extracted from Ringland (1999). It is published by permission of Elsevier Science. It describes some of the ways in which futures thinking may be flawed, or be excellent but fail to influence the organization.

BELIEVING WHAT WE WANT TO BELIEVE AND NOT PAYING ATTENTION

Historical data (Figure II.4.1) showed that oil-drilling activity had been growing for a number of years and, naturally, the oil-drilling business had expanded in that time. When forecasts of the future were made, including "high", "medium" and "low" activity, they simply reflected the belief that growth would continue. The forecasters believed what they wanted to believe. However, in fact, oil drilling collapsed soon after this forecast, because there was a change in the US tax laws, which effectively weakened the financial incentives to drill. Could the forecasters have foreseen this change in the law? Given the number of lobbyists who inhabit Washington, DC, early signs of a changing law were probably visible, but there was a clear failure of attention. This graph therefore illustrates two failures:

- believing what we want to believe;

- a failure of attention.

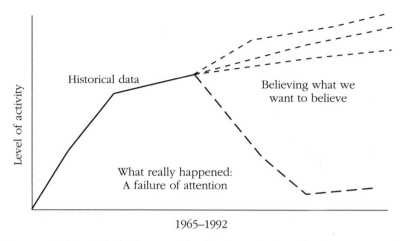

Figure II.4.1 Oil drilling activity in the USA (Ringland, 1999; reproduced by permission of Elsevier Science).

THE TYRANNY OF THE PRESENT

Another reason we have trouble foreseeing what will happen in the future is that our views of the future are always coloured by our most recent experience. This is well illustrated in Figure II.4.2, but was also apparent during consultancy work in Asia in 1996 when I repeatedly asked workshop participants: "What could go wrong in Asia? What will cause growth to slow? Could we have a financial crisis in Asia?" After 20 years of growth and stability, the universal answer in 1996 was: "That is not possible." This is another example of the tyranny of the present.

ASKING THE RIGHT QUESTION

One of the ways to get around the tyranny of the present is to ask a contrarian question – something that forces us to think differently about the present. Right questions, though, are often hard to find. They often appear only when we distance ourselves from what everyone is saying about a subject and find some empty space

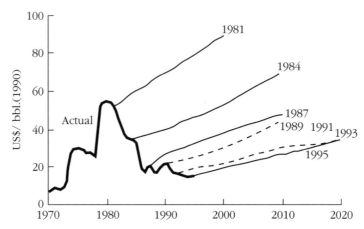

Figure II.4.2 Crude-oil price forecasts (Ringland, 1999; reproduced by permission of Elsevier Science; source: International Energy Workshop).

we cannot explain. These empty spaces are fruitful sources of right questions that need to be asked if we want a good view of the future.

OVERESTIMATING OUR ABILITY TO CONTROL THE FUTURE – "WE CAN HANDLE IT"

Another reason we get our forecasts wrong is that we assume our organizations are strong enough to cope with change. In two assignments with very different, but confident companies, the working groups wrote descriptions of the world their companies would be facing. They were complacent views of worlds in which the companies were bound to succeed and overcome any obstacles. When asked what name they would give to this future, each group responded: "We can handle it." This belief means that only a very quick and superficial look at the future is likely to be undertaken – and is also likely to be wrong.

THE NEED TO PRESENT A POINT OF VIEW – THE EXAMPLE OF HIV/AIDS

When the AIDS epidemic was first discovered, doctors and epidemiologists realized that they were facing an incurable disease that could spread for many years, infecting many people long before illness was visible. They also knew that there were many uncertainties about the spread of the disease that made it genuinely difficult to know how far the virus would spread through any particular population. Equally, the experts quickly learned that using condoms, practising safe sex, sterilizing needles and blood supplies, etc. could slow the spread of HIV down. However, this meant persuading many people to alter their behaviour. To help convince people to change their behaviour, the uncertainties about projections of the spread of the disease were underplayed and risks were highlighted. Later, when the disease did not spread as anticipated in several cultures (e.g. the UK), the risks remained, but the overdramatization of the spread of the epidemic made many people question whether the epidemiologists were right about the need to change their behaviour. In this case, the very real public health need to present a point of view forced the forecasters to develop a highly dramatic case that minimized the equally relevant uncertainties in their forecasts.

THE UNRELIABILITY OF EXPERTS – OR THE VALUE OF INNOCENT EYES

In the mid to late 1980s, I was working with a company on the future of Japan. At the time, I was struck by the the mindless repetition from business people interviewed that "Japan is different" – a cultural explanation for difficulties my Western business clients were discovering. The most frequent aspects of difference that were cited were (a) "consensus is important in Japan" and (b) "the Japanese take the long term-point of view". As the project proceeded, I began to wonder what the basis of consensus was and why it was upheld. I also wondered how the Japanese paid for the long-term view and discovered a number of very interesting rules in the financial system that made it possible to support long-term business strategies. So, I organized two meetings of experts. In one meeting, I asked people to discuss the question: "When will the consensus in Japan break down". In the other meeting, I asked: "What will happen as the Japanese financial system opens to the outside world?" I was given two clear answers: "The consensus won't break down, Japan is different," and "There will be a smooth convergence of the Japanese and international financial systems."

Neither conclusion has been supported by events since the late 1980s. So, why were the experts wrong? Perhaps, when they are expert in another culture they take on the myths and beliefs of that culture, making it more difficult for them to see the weaknesses that are there. As a non-expert, I did not question their conclusions, but it has since turned out that my "ignorant" questions were closer to the future than the expert views. This kind of experience has led several of us to rethink "the value of innocent eyes" in forcing us to question the automatic conclusions experts often offer.

TIME TO DO A GOOD ANALYSIS

One of the reasons for relying on experts is that very few organizations take the time or devote the resources needed to collect and understand the relevant facts. Deadlines are tight, staff are already overworked and there is no budget for commissioning outside research. Even when the budget is there, research that helps us to understand the future tends to ask different questions than those asked either by operational people or by academics. As a result, ordinary research skills are often not enough, while the skills involved in researching what will happen in the future are scarce and undervalued. As a result, good analysis is just not done. An example of this came during 1996 when there was a clear need to gain a better understanding of Asian financial systems, but no organizations that year had the budget, time or skills to undertake such work.

ASSUMPTIONS AND THE ILLUSION OF CERTAINTY

Assumptions about the future are intrinsically necessary. We must be able to assume that the ground will be under our feet before we take a single step. And yet, our assumptions can cause us trouble because they lie deeply hidden in our beliefs and behaviours. They can also conceal ignorance. In one training exercise where we were working on the future of rural Scotland, the group assumed for two days that people in rural Scotland worked as fishermen, farmers, foresters and in other rural activities. However, when we looked at employment and government expenditures, we discovered that in fact over 50 per cent of the population was directly dependent on government money – either as unemployment benefits, pensions or salaries. It is examples like this one that show how our assumptions and their illusion of certainty can lead our forecasts astray.

A QUESTION OF TIMING

Another frequent source of error is to make an accurate prediction about what will happen in the future, but to get the timing wrong. For many people, the Club of Rome's *Limits to Growth* (Meadows et al., 1992) was completely wrong, because their predictions were not fulfilled when the authors said they would be fulfilled. But has that made those predictions wrong? I doubt it. Instead, it is a question of timing. Figure II.4.3 illustrates the problem.

"IT TAKES 30 YEARS TO GET A GOOD IDEA ACCEPTED"

Even when we get everything right – the right question, good analysis, right timing – our forecasts may still not be good because they cannot gain acceptance. One of the interesting things about working in this field for the past 15 years is seeing how long it takes for ideas to take hold among groups. There seems to be an instinctive rejection of a novel view of the future. For instance, a speaker gave a talk about importing wheat into the Middle East, in which he described it as "virtual water", since the

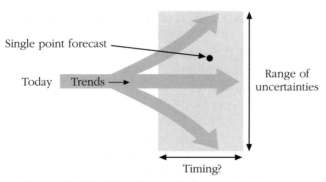

Single point forecast

Today   Trends →

Range of
uncertainties

Timing?

Figure II.43 The danger in forecasting is ...

water needed to grow wheat is embodied in the wheat imports. Thirty years ago, the very idea of importing wheat into the Middle East was rejected because countries believed they needed to be self-sufficient in food production, even though they did not have enough water to meet this objective. Now, importing wheat is accepted practice – hence the speaker's conclusion that "it takes 30 years for a good idea to be accepted."

OBEDIENCE VS. CURIOSITY

Another reason our forecasts go wrong is that we want to write a good diagnostic view of how the world works and where it might be going, but worry that our bosses will not accept such an analysis. We therefore water down and temper our conclusions. I was particularly aware of this tension while working in Asia, where there is a strong culture of obedience and conformity. In this culture, curiosity can be confused with disloyalty. But this is not a problem limited to Asian cultures; it exists in many Western corporations where people are promoted based on their ability to echo, rather than question, the views at the top. Hence, many of our forecasts are wrong because of this tension between obedience and curiosity.

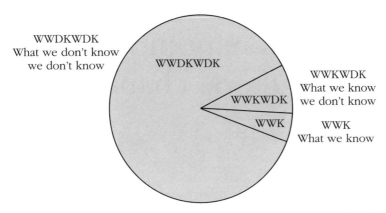

Figure II.4.4 What we don't know (Michael, 1973; reproduced by permission of Jossey-Bass).

WHAT WE DON'T KNOW WE DON'T KNOW

Finally, there is a very good reason we get our forecasts wrong: our knowledge is very limited. Figure II.4.4 (from Michael, 1973) is a metaphor for understanding the importance of this circle of knowledge and ignorance. The fact is we are unable to know all that it would be useful to know. Even if we include our knowledge of what we don't know, most of what we need to know is outside our comprehension. We don't even know it is there. That means that we are always making forecasts in a state of ignorance and uncertainty. Inevitably, some of our forecasts will be wrong.

SECTION II.5

Evolutionary models for cultural change

Civilization as we know it has seen an enormous amount of change – social, cultural, scientific, economic, political – and the 20th century alone has seen a significant proportion of these transitions, so much so that our ways of thinking and lifestyles are transforming faster than ever. To adapt to this, we need scenarios that embrace the future instead of focusing on the past. Glen Hiemstra outlines models that can assist scenario planners in the changing world. He is founder and CEO of Futurist.com, ghiemstra@futurist.com. *This article was first published in* Scenario and Strategy Planning *in October 2001 and is published here with the permission of* Risk Management Bulletin.

SCENARIOS EXPLORE THE FUTURE

Success in scenario planning depends on being able to look at the future in the future's own terms. At the core of scenario planning is the intent to let go of the assumptions about current reality that dominate our strategic thinking. The intent is instead to open us to alternate assumptions through a rigorous, yet open-ended examination of alternative futures.

This is in contrast to many traditional approaches to strategic planning. A standard approach is to begin with current reality, and then to extrapolate trends into the future based on assumptions that there will be more of some things and less of others. For example, there will be more people and less oil in the future. Having made our predictions, we fashion strategies to respond to what we predict. But the result can often be an elegant plan for a more efficient past, rather than a truly new future.

In the new century, all planners are aware that mere extrapolation of current trends is insufficient to enable breakthrough thinking about strategy. Planners are generally aware that we live in a time of discontinuous change. As Alvin Toffler once put it:

> *Most people still seem unaware that the basic rules are changing. It means re-evaluating issues in new terms. The straight-line future runs flat into a wall.*

Good scenarios are a way of penetrating and challenging hidden assumptions, but good scenarios depend on understanding the larger context of the future. To understand this context, one must ask good questions, beginning with: "What is your image of the future?"

EXAMINING THE FUTURE: MODELS

The question is deceptively simple, and one might counter that all scenarios are an attempt to answer the question. At one level, that is true. In any particular case, however, in which scenario planners are developing a range of plausible futures, each plausible scenario will be set in a larger context of assumptions about change. Asking the image question in its largest scope is vital to establishing a plausible context for alternative scenarios. Asking the question in its largest scope is vital then to seeing the future in the future's own terms.

Where does one begin? We would argue that, despite the obvious reality of discontinuous change, there is fundamental value in looking back in order to grasp very large patterns of evolution or change. We offer two models, both of which have explanatory and predictive power to see the future.

The first model deals with the dimensionality of civilizations, in terms of the number of physical dimensions in which a civilization lives and moves (Knoke, 1996).

Dot-based culture

As we currently understand human history, from a time as long as two million years ago until as recently as 5,000 years ago, humankind lived in a world of zero dimensions. That is, they lived in "dot-based" culture. Hunter–gatherer, nomadic peoples lived in exceptionally small groups, usually only a few families. A group as large as 50 was rare. They moved about within a limited area in search of game and edible plants, but generally did not move far. Such peoples certainly were aware of three dimensions, as everything they saw had height, width and depth. But they lived in fixed dots, or zero dimensions. In fact, it is likely that they generally avoided contact with other dots, such contact being potentially dangerous. In a lifetime, one might see only a few hundred other people.

One-dimensional civilization

Dot-based civilization began to evolve about 15,000 years ago, as a warmer climate enabled farming of plants and animals. Dot-based bands began to gather in larger groups, eventually in permanent villages. By about 3,000 years ago, the transition was complete in much of the world, and nomads had become farmers and village dwellers.

More importantly, first adventurers, then merchants began to establish fixed trade routes between the permanent settlements. The "amber route" evolved in Europe, the "silk road" connected China, India and Europe. Camel caravans crossed deserts, and ships began to sail along the coastlines. Travel was one-dimensional, following fixed routes between dots.

Villages grew into great trading cities, and wealth grew in an unprecedented way. Not only goods were exchanged. Knowledge and ideas were exchanged, and learning began to flourish. Civilization had become one-dimensional, a culture of social interaction along fixed paths.

Two-dimensional civilization

Eventually, trade routes began to cross and overlap, and people began to develop a two-dimensional sense of the world. They thought about the width and length of the world, even speculating on its shape and whether the world had an end. The first two-dimensional maps of the world were drawn. A concept of society emerged in which people in villages in every direction were considered part of the whole. Leaders of great trading centres saw an opportunity to accumulate wealth and power by using the roads to grab control of vast territories, and empires were born.

Shipping expanded, and then ushered in the full transition to a two-dimensional culture in about the 15th century. Shipbuilders discovered how to build large ships seaworthy enough and with technology that enabled them to sail close to the wind and out of sight of land. The "age of discovery" that resulted wrote the concluding chapter of civilization's shift to two dimensions. Within a short 35-year span, European ships rounded the Horn of Africa, reached the Americas, and sailed around the world.

This new power in two dimensions led within five centuries to a world in which 25 nations in Europe held a tight grip on 84 per cent of the world's land mass. Evolution into two dimensions was complete, and humankind was in an era of free travel over the earth's surface.

Three-dimensional civilization
Even as the two-dimensional world reached completion, adventurers began to experiment with movement in the third dimension. For two centuries, people attempted to fly using primitive balloons and gliders. Then, just one thousand days into the twentieth century, powered flight became a reality. Within a dozen years, aeroplanes were being used in warfare. Passenger service followed soon after. By 1950, 20 million people took commercial flights, and, by 2000, over a billion were flying each year. Rockets launched people and satellites into the more distant third dimension. The emergence of three-dimensional culture again spawned new social and political orders, and humanity even began to conceive of the earth itself as a spaceship travelling in three dimensions.

Comparing the civilizations
Understanding the common themes within this framework gives an enhanced ability to see the future. One-dimensional civilization

lasted about 5,000 years, beginning with recorded civilization. Two-dimensional civilization lasted about 500 years, culminating with the great conquest of the seas. Three-dimensional civilization has lasted about a century, and has been dominant for about 50 years. So change accelerates.

In addition, cultures do not move in lock step together along this evolutionary path. Even today, there are peoples effectively living in one dimension, others in two and others in three. Each new dimension increases the degree of freedom and action, and generates unpredictable new opportunities; wealth, learning and power accumulate to those who move into the higher dimension.

Finally, in each shift of dimensions, it would have appeared at the outset that the suppliers of the tools of new dimension would become the wealth leaders. But it is not so. Rather, it is the users of the tools of the new dimension that eventually emerge as the new wealth leaders. Thus, it was not the carpenters and ship-builders of the age of discovery that became the wealthiest, but rather the users of these ships. Likewise, the suppliers of oil to three-dimensional civilization become wealthy indeed, but it is the users of this tool who generate the greatest wealth and opportunity.

Four-dimensional civilization

Now, we have begun the move into a fourth dimension, the dimension of cyberspace. The move began decades ago, but is even now in its adolescence. The world of cyberspace provides even greater degrees of freedom and action, and will again redefine wealth, learning and power. This is a world of four dimensions, and no dimensions, a world of instant communication across any distance, and a world of no distance at all. If the shift plays out in a way similar to those that have come before, new orders of wealth, learning, information and power will once again emerge. We might also assume that this change will be accelerated.

The year 2000

Is there evidence that we have entered the fourth dimension? Few will argue with this assertion, but for those who wonder, consider the following list of developments in the year 2000, which historians will point to as evidence of the shift toward the fourth dimension:

- e-commerce became major force in business, even as the web caught its breath;

- data traffic instead of the voice became driving force in telecommunications;

- mobile phones in Japan, Nordic and Latin countries exceeded land line phones;

- optical storage technology accelerated rapidly;

- distributed computing fundamentally altered how we thought about computing;

- the working draft of human genome was finished;

- scientists produced the quantum computer and the DNA computer;

- Clay Ford forecast that fuel cells would replace internal combustion;

- advances in quantum physics became the dominant force in technological development.

The year 2025

By the year 2025, developments we now consider to be wildcards will quite likely have come to fruition, as living in four dimensions speeds up the exchange of knowledge and learning:

- We live in a data-flow culture, in which all transistors are connected to all other transistors in one vast global computer. Plugged in, we cannot imagine an unplugged world.

- Nanoscale replicators have begun to make earlier forms of manufacturing obsolete.

- Light-based and molecular computing are realities, making the limits of silicon moot.

- Genomics has moved fully beyond research and development into biogenetic treatments.

- Anti-ageing has radically extended the average lifespan.

The dimensionality of the evolution of civilization, then, provides one framework for considering the future in the future's own terms.

THE TECHNO–SOCIAL–ECONOMIC REVOLUTION

A second framework is equally compelling. It is the framework of the techno–social–economic revolution. In this way of looking at evolutionary futures, the fundamental equation revolves around technological innovations that have the capacity to change everything, and thus lead to a revolution in how we conduct our social and economic lives.

While such revolutions have happened many times historically, the last one occurred a century ago, when telephones, electricity and the automobile joined forces during the final industrial revolution. That shift is also known as the electromechanical revolution. This story, while familiar, is rarely focused on in terms of just how fast things changed for people living in industrialized regions at that time. Within about 50 years, everything changed: how we make things, how we buy and sell things, how, when and where we work, how and where we live in relation to our work, how we communicate, how and when we travel, and so on. All of these factors fundamentally changed.

The process of such a revolution can be compared with the popping of popcorn. The first kernels pop with the initial inventions. Those inventions of significance generate small industries.

Older industries begin to flatten out, a few to die. The new industries begin to interconnect and reinforce each other. More popcorn begins popping. About 30 years after the initial inventions, the new industries are sufficiently mature to emerge as the dominant ones, generating the most wealth, employing more and more people. All the popcorn begins popping at once, and everywhere you look it seems that enterprises are changing, as the social economy begins to shift. During the final 20 years or so of a period of about 50 years, an avalanche of change occurs as all the popcorn pours into the bowl.

The current techno–social–economic revolution began in 1971 when Intel sold the first silicon chip. It accelerated through the personal computer revolution, the introduction of fibre optics and mobile phones to telecommunications, the emergence of biotechnology, the development of the World Wide Web from the early Internet, the completion of the Human Genome Project and finally the creation of the first commercial nanotechnology companies. Thus, the current revolution might be seen by historians as a revolution of digital, bio and nanotechnology.

THE DIGITAL REVOLUTION

Digital technology is advancing, as we all know, by growth curves that exhibit doubling times from 18 months for computer chips, to 12 months for information storage, to 7 months for the capacity of telecommunications. There is good reason to believe that these doubling times will continue apace until 2020, when we approach human intelligence in machines that cost about US$1,000. We will awaken to find that, very quietly, we have ceased to be the brightest things on earth, by some measure of brightness.

Furthermore, these machines, and their transistors, will be completely integrated into a vast digital network – a global computer if you will – in which every transistor may communicate with every other transistor. We will be able to walk into a room, look at a very large flat screen on the wall, and say: "I would like Mount Everest," and a real-time video image of sunset on Mount Everest will become the view.

The critical question to be addressed is how to bring this tremendous bandwidth to the mind. The current technology we use, screens and keyboards, will not suffice.

BIOTECHNOLOGY

Genomics, or biotechnology, will flourish in the next 25 years. As both diagnostic and treatment techniques are perfected, we'll see longer and healthier lifespans. The most critical questions will be ones of ethics about how far we should go, and ones of equity about how shall the benefits of genomics be brought to the whole human family.

NANOTECHNOLOGY

Nanotechnology – the science of manufacturing at the molecular or atomic level – may in the end change the future most of all. Currently, our manufacturing techniques, while considered advanced, do not differ all that much from the ancient ways. We combine trillions of molecules by cooking them and then pouring the results into moulds. We might machine the final product further by scraping it. Nanotechnology holds out the promise of precisely manipulating and combining basic atoms or molecules, leading to materials that are not only extremely small, but also stronger, lighter and more flexible than anything that exists today.

Within a few years, the nanotech material known as carbon-60, or nanotubes, will be produced in quantities of tons per year, rather than the experimental amounts of 2001. Nearer to the year 2020, exponential assemblers may enable mass production with nanotechnology. If an exponential assembler is perfected, manufacturing will face a revolution as fast and thorough as that of the final industrial revolution of a century earlier.

SOCIAL AND CULTURAL CHANGES TO 2025

When we look back from the perspective of 2025 using this framework, what will be the social cultural changes we might see?

Work life

Work will have shifted from jobs to stints. Rather than work being organized around career tracks and wages and benefits, work will be increasingly organized around the short term, the project and self-managed employment.

Retirement as conceived of (and actually invented) in the 20th century will be seen as a memory. Retirement in the 20th century meant that after a period of income-generating work, a short period of elderly life would be devoted to leisure and paid for by accumulated benefits. By 2025, a reinvention of the third phase of life formerly called retirement will be complete.

Home life

Homes will have been reinvented to be more like they were for most of human history, the centre of life. Rather than the 20th century model in which homes became a place to eat a meal, sleep and store personal possessions, homes will again have become a place to do some learning, some work, some health care, some entertaining and so on.

Education

Learning will no longer be confined to schoolhouses, as it was at the beginning in the mid-nineteenth century. Rather, learning will take place both in schools and in cyberspace, as hybrid "cyber schools" become the norm.

Government

Finally, the 20th century worldwide move toward big government being the institution relied upon to tackle large social problems will have completed a shift to other institutions. The great thinker on the future, Peter Drucker, argues that growing non-profit enterprises will take on the role of dealing with large social problems.

OTHER SOURCES OF CHANGE

The two broad conceptual frameworks presented here for understanding cultural change – first a dimensional view of civilization, and second a techno-revolutionary view – each offer a tool for knowing where we are going. Various plausible scenarios can be embedded within these frameworks, with an enhanced probability that the scenario creators can know where we are going, and thus effectively challenge their current reality-based assumptions.

They are not, however, the whole story regarding contexts for future scenarios and cultural change. Additional developments such as the rapid growth of air travel and resultant explosive growth in worldwide tourism and movement, the shift to alternate energy sources, the emergence of new automobiles with hybrid or perhaps fuel cell engines just in time to combat global warming, and mobile robots are all part of the next 25 years.

But no development matches up to the last cultural change one must account for in future scenarios. It is a development so surprising, and for most people still so counter-intuitive, that it is likely to be overlooked. The development can be captured in the following image. Sometime between the years 2015 and 2020, perhaps much sooner, a global conference is going to convene to consider the question: "What shall the global community do about the impending decline in the human population?"

POPULATION DECLINE

For centuries, the human population has grown ever faster. It is an unexamined assumption for many that human population growth will outstrip the planet's ability to support the human community. It is only now being noticed that rapid population growth is coming to an end, not because of disease or catastrophe, but because of economic security, which is tightly coupled with decreases in fertility rates. Only four countries in the world have seen their birth rates increase since 1980, three of which are Scandinavian countries with birth rates still below that needed for population replacement. Whole regions of the world have fallen below birth rates necessary for even zero population growth.

Now a study has emerged that forecasts that the human population is likely to go over the top at a number much lower than previously thought: at 8.8 billion. It is even increasingly possible that the human population in 2100 will be smaller than the population of 2001 (Lutz et al., 2001).

No development that we can think of will have a more profound impact on culture than a shift to declining, not to mention ageing, populations. This future reality is imminent for much of Western Europe, Japan, China, Russia, Canada and elsewhere. The debate on how to sustain economies in the face of fewer people, and religious and national pressures to have or not have more children, will be intense. Scenario-based examination of this issue is urgent.

CONCLUSION

What is your image of the future? This is the question for scenarios. Historical perspective, evolutionary frameworks, technology developments and population trends are all concepts to account for in constructing useful scenarios. To anticipate the future in the future's terms, it is always helpful to keep in mind a final concept. As we understand the history of the universe, everything possible today was at one time impossible. If this is true, then everything impossible today may at some time in the future be possible. In the end, the future is not something that just happens to us. The future is something we do.

Where next?

This section discusses some of the major fault lines facing us, and suggests that the challenges of harnessing technology will be among those needing a visionary approach. It also outlines the change in use of scenarios, from their association with corporate planning to knowledge management tools and ways of creating shared understanding.

A PERIOD OF DRAMATIC CHANGE

We are clearly in the middle of a period of dramatic change. For instance:

- See Samuel Huntington's seminal work on the change from a two-centre balance of power in the Cold War to a position in which fractures run on cultural lines, not those of national boundaries (Huntington, 1989). He particularly flagged the likelihood of population increases in Muslim countries leading to the rise of aggressive Islamic fundamentalism, terrorism and the possibility of a new Cold or even Hot War.

- Ervin Laszlo's *Vision 2020* (Laszlo, 1994) is subtitled "Re-ordering chaos for global survival" and takes as given that the changes facing us are massive. The question is: What strategies will allow us to cope?

- Watts Wacker in *The 500 Year Delta* (Taylor *et al.*, 1997) sees convergence of a number of changes, with the power of the producers of goods decreasing and that of consumers increasing.

- John Petersen in his *Road to 2015* (Petersen, 1994) sees that information technology plus new ideas and technologies in science, plus the saturation of the planet will cause a global paradigm shift similar to that seen in the West in the 15th and 16th centuries.

- Peter Schwartz in *The Long Boom* (Schwartz et al., 1999) anticipates three major waves of change: from the Internet, from biotechnology and from low-cost energy. The book flags the increasing differential between the USA, particularly California, and Europe/Asia/Latin America.

- Kevin Kelly in *New Rules for the New Economy* (Kelly, 1999) discusses new rules for the economy, driven by the decreasing cost of networking and decreasing transaction costs, in a globalizing world where pervasive information has the effect of making the individual less constrained and increasingly aware of new opportunities and options.

- The next generation of information technology will be pervasive. Embedded devices will raise new legal, regulatory, ethical and moral issues for society. Intelligent devices will communicate with other intelligent devices. Who will police their trading? Bill Joy (www.zdnet.com) has speculated that we are already beyond the point of no return in our efforts to control our environment.

THE FUTURE OF SCENARIO THINKING

Several strands are emerging from the thinkers in scenarios. I acknowledge here discussions with Clem Bezold, Adrian Davies, Tony Hodgson, Rolf Jensen and Oliver Sparrow (Oxbrow et al., 2001) among many others, a paper by van Notten and Rotmans (2001) and the Harvard Business Review Management Update (2000).

Scenarios as knowledge-management tools

The work to create scenarios incorporates defining and assessing the most important forces and systems for the organization. So, scenarios provide a structured model or models of the world. They provide a way to organize the many action points, concerns and bullet points that managers accumulate, ranking issues in importance and in timeliness. The variables that underpin the operating environment are the likely sources of uncertainty and of competitive positioning.

If the variables can be used as axes on a matrix, then the matrix is a visual aid for the organization to discuss likely directions of change in positioning – their own and competitors. This is why the map of two independent dimensions is such a useful tool, with often a scenario moving across the map with time. The discussion of the speed and scope of change is made easier by seeing the underlying factors on the map. One example, from Ringland (1997), shows possible migration paths for the South African economy (Figure II.6.1).

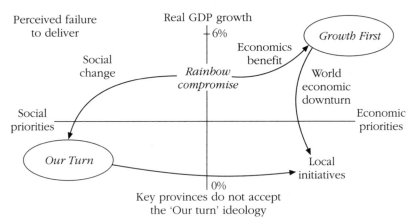

Figure II.6.1 Migration paths for South Africa (published with permission of John Wiley & Sons, Ltd; source: United Distillers).

Once an organization has established scenarios and communicated them widely, they will start to be used as part of the vocabulary for defining paradigms – shortcuts to understanding. The strategy of the organization has a context and a framework within which options can be developed. People can anticipate better what new initiatives will be welcomed and what business directions will become viable and which wither away. This is a definition of empowerment in an organization that is competent.

Short-termism and vision in a time of high uncertainty

The in-house development of complex scenarios founded on extensive new desk research does not fit with many current corporate styles and timescales. Some organizations use pre-existing scenarios as starting points for their own tailored versions for use in planning or discussion. See the discussion of "Off the shelf scenarios" in Part III.

Others concentrate on the development of visionary scenarios specific to the organization, incorporating their values and mission, to provide a framework for later work to develop implementation routes, as discussed earlier.

The presentation of these scenarios is often as a story or narrative, theatre or video (see de Geus, 1999 or Allan et al., 2002).

One technique for linking short-term decision making into scenarios is via intelligence (see "Linking scenarios into the organization" in Part III).

Scenarios as thinking tools

The process of developing scenarios is one of the few management team activities more likely to create synergy than to promote rivalry. It does this by providing:

- a shared environment for the surfacing and discussion of assumptions – most teams have members who have arrived through a variety of routes, experiences and therefore default assumptions;

113

- a forum for exploring the deep structure of the industry or competitive environment by thinking through the dynamics of driving forces and actions;

- a possibility of exploring alternative mindsets, whether in relation to future events and worlds or the current position.

GO BOLDLY . . .

A strong theme running through scenario work today is vision, or "where do you want to be?" Glen Hiemstra (see www.futurist.com) uses three keys to anticipating the future:

- Is it technologically feasible?

- Is it economically viable (when)?

- Is it socially/politically desirable?

Conclusions

Part II has the aim of providing checklists and pointers to help ensure that the content of scenarios is robust, by discussing structural assumptions, trends and pitfalls.

In creating scenarios for use in an organization, it is important to:

- Realize the new environment for strategy and scenarios, in which the creation of vision to allow distributed, dispersed and empowered organizations to act coherently is a key requirement.

- Relate the major axes of uncertainty to the questions facing the organization. Section II.2 suggests outlines for the strategic questions facing many organizations.

- Understand that scenarios will build on a number of known factors likely to define the future, with uncertainties arising in the political, economic or social arenas; it is important that these "known" factors are well researched and understood. Sections II.3 and II.5 suggest some trends that have major effects and warn us about frequently found hurdles to forecasting the future.

- Be realistic – the best scenarios may fall on stony ground. Section II.4 suggests some common reasons and ways of ensuring that scenarios are heard and acted on.

Section II.6 highlights a number of applications of scenarios outside the planning field; for instance, as:

- knowledge-management tools, providing a framework for under-standing the current environment;

- scenarios as thinking tools, to bring assumptions to the surface, to explore alternative mindsets, to develop a common vocabulary in a management team;

- scenarios to create vision for the organization, and to explore how to achieve the vision.

PART III

MAKING SCENARIOS WORK

SUMMARY

This part contains a number of checklists and dos and don'ts aimed at facilitating the successful use of scenarios by managers.

Section III.1 is "The environment for scenario thinking", covering factors such as timing, the human dimension and whether the aims of the manager can be accomplished by using an existing scenario set.

Section III.2 is a guide to the overall process, and Section III.3 is a guide to the practicalities of getting started. If it reads like a project management guide, it is!

Section III.4 is one of the key sections about deciding the question – often the outcome of initial interviews. Section III.5 covers more practical detail such as interviews and workshops, and the role of tools.

Section III.6 describes the mechanics of scenario creation, discusses "how many scenarios" need to be created and gives guidelines for developing the storyline.

Section III.7 covers the crucial "scenarios to plans" stage, and Section III.8 discusses linking scenarios into the organization: techniques for communication, and aligning with the organization's research and intelligence operations.

Section III.9 summarizes the main points and lessons learned, and concludes that "Scenarios are part of strategic management: their use rather than their existence is the key to success".

The environment for scenario thinking

A scenarios project will be successful if people make decisions that are influenced by it. Some of the factors that increase the chances of success are listed, as are some sources of publicly available scenarios that may be an alternative to in-house development. Scenario thinking can be a part of an organization's armoury in a number of situations. This section pulls out some generally applicable pointers to a suitable environment. The subsections "Engaging stakeholders" and "Adapting the scenarios" are reproduced from Berkhout (2001) with the permission of Crown Copyright.

WHY SCENARIOS?

Scenarios are now accepted as a management tool. Where is their use best focused?

- Scenarios are indicated where the force of the external world requires senior managers to think "outside-in" – as in times of structural change in the environment, industry, competitors or customers.

- Scenarios provide an environment for creating a shared context and language inside the organization. This is important in an environment where specialists or people from different cultures or departments need to contribute to solving a shared problem and implementing the solution.

119

Scenarios are possible futures. If well chosen for the organization, they will encapsulate worlds that have very different answers to the significant questions facing the organization. They give a forward-looking rather than a historical framework to decisions on investment, market intelligence, new products and markets, and portfolio management. Many organizations additionally flag other benefits of scenarios; for example:

- Creating a common language; many scenario thinkers today believe that the most significant outcomes of scenario projects are a sense of vision, allowing the organization to pull together to implement it.

- Creating a cadre of people with strategic thinking capability and a network across the organization.

- Allowing teams to cooperate on issues outside the operational time frame, with consequent reduction in tensions from current roles. By focusing on a horizon, defensive attitudes to current responsibilities are less relevant. Would you expect to be doing the same job in 10 years' time?

BEFORE YOU START

Engaging stakeholders
The key challenge of the scenario planning process is to engage stakeholders inside and outside the organization. It can only be successful in promoting creative and unconventional thinking if the process is based on engagement and trustful relations. However, the usefulness of the scenario planning method is sometimes contested. Thinking 10, 20 or more years ahead is not routine for most organizations and can seem difficult or meaningless. Scenarios are also criticized because the underlying assumptions can rarely be validated and are to some extent a matter of judgement. Scientists often express concerns about using an inherently subjective framework in the context of research. Practitioners

sometimes feel that a scenario exercise does not generate sufficient tangible outcomes:

- Engaging stakeholders requires, first of all, clarity about the aims and limitations of the approach. Scenarios are not aiming to predict the future, or not even to identify the most likely future. Instead, they map out a "possibility space" to inform the decisions of the present. The scenarios method is based on subjective choices (as in fact is any other approach to explore uncertain futures), but, unlike other tools, it allows stakeholders to discuss and challenge these judgements.

- If participants are to be convinced of the importance of their contribution, the aim of the scenario planning process needs to be well-defined and clear indications need to be given as to how the results of will feed into decision making.

The time needs to be right
The outcomes of the project should be ready to feed into the organization's thinking when the organization is asking for directions into the future: scenarios for South Africa were created to influence the political process leading to the seminal elections in 1994. In other projects, timing may depend on the availability of participants.

It is not a good time:

- when the organization is very unstable at decision-making levels;

- if the results will be available just after a major strategic planning round has completed and set for implementation;

- if the organization is in panic mode.

It is a good time:

- Just after a new appointment at strategic levels.

- If timing allows the scenario outputs to be input to a strategic planning round.

- If the organization is facing specific challenges such as:
  - the chaotic environment makes it difficult to see the emerging patterns of competition or cooperation;
  - the organization faces specific decisions – the question is known but the answers are hotly debated;
  - business plans are not being met – maybe some of the underlying assumptions are no longer valid;
  - culture change in traditional markets is threatening;
  - new initiatives are competing for attention and money, and a choice has to be made;
  - a conglomerate is finding that its component businesses seem incompatible – what are the default scenarios of each?

Get the organizational framework straight
Who is the client?

- Does he or she have access to budget and is the first stage underpinned by clarity of purpose?

- What is the reporting structure?

- If consultants are used, are they working *for* the project team or *with* the project team?

- Are there opponents to the project – beware of hidden agendas?

- Identifying the first manager to work with in applying the scenarios is a good preliminary step; in fact, a preliminary project focused on his or her needs may be a useful introduction.

Scope and deliverables

Be sure to understand what is needed and when:

- Is the scope of the study, coupled with the deliverables, timescale and support (e.g. research staff), clear?

- The people who will do the work should be identified early on: secondees from around the organization are ideal, and outside consultants are a great help in giving the project status and in facilitating the process.

- Deciding the timescale for your scenarios. For example, "Scenarios for Scotland in 2010" for a project completed in 1999 is a significant choice of date in that the new Scottish Parliament would have been in place 10 years by then, posing the questions: What does Scotland want the Parliament to achieve? What does Scotland want to be?

DO YOU NEED TO CREATE SCENARIOS?

An important early decision is whether to create specific scenarios for the organization or to base the scenario thinking around existing scenarios. The case studies in Section I.6 of ICL using the Chatham House Forum scenarios and the Trading Group in Section IV.8 illustrate how existing scenarios can be strong contenders for exposing issues. Using pre-existing scenarios as a basis for work in an organization – or country – makes a lot of sense under some circumstances; for example:

- where the external environment is a dominant factor (e.g. the economy), use scenarios that are based on extensive desk research on economic futures;

- where the intention is to introduce scenario thinking to a group of people, without the investment in time to research and build specific scenarios;

123

- where many of the same considerations apply to all departments in a company, and where a business unit wants to explore alternative futures.

Which to choose and where to find them
The sources in Table III.1.1 are all in the public domain. Section III.5 gives an agenda for a workshop using existing scenarios.

Adapting the scenarios
The scenarios in Table III.1.1 provide a generic framework but they will require extending when working with specific groups on their business issues. This requires:

- identification of key drivers in the sector (e.g. international markets, social preferences);

- an assessment of the links between drivers and relevant sectoral trends;

- specialist knowledge of the sector.

The scenario framework is a flexible tool that should be adapted and altered to suit the needs of a given study; they can be modified and "played with". The benefit of using a common set of basic dimensions within an organization is that cross-departmental initiatives and discussions are easier. However, these dimensions may not be relevant, or there may be an interest in testing alternatives. New dimensions and new scenario labels would then be the right course to take.

Producing four scenario elaborations can be time consuming, with diminishing returns for the effort. One alternative is to choose a smaller number of scenarios for in-depth analysis (say two or three scenarios). Some studies have chosen to look at diametrically opposed scenarios (e.g. *Islamic experiments* and *Charismatic technocracy* in Section IV.1). However, Berkhout recommends that the symmetric approach to scenario elaboration is retained during the first phase to avoid the risk of narrowing down the thinking too early.

Table III.1.1 Sources of scenarios

Sources of scenarios	Timescale	Topic	Website or ISBN
Richard Baldock	2008	Organizations	0-471-98462-0
Chatham House Forum	2015	Economy of the industrialized world	www.chforum.org
CIA	2015	Global trends	www.cia.gov/cia/ publications/ globaltrends2015
Coates and Jarrett	2025	US and global society	www.coatesandjarrett.com
UK Foresight	2020	Environmental	www.foresight.gov.uk
Glen Peters	2015	Customers	0-273-62417-2
John L. Peterson	2015	Security	1-878-72985-9
Gill Ringland	2005	Information and communications technology	0-471-97790-X
ScMI	2010	Global manufacturing	www.scmi.de
Shell	2050	Energy needs, choices and possibilities	www.shell.com
Singapore	2004	Trade, technology and tribe	www.gov.sg
World Business Council for Sustainable Development	2050	Sustainable development	www.wbcsd.ch
WIRED	2020	Commercial life	www.wired.com/wired/ scenarios

Effort devoted to the development of indicators will vary between studies. Indicators may be illustrative of the storylines, or they may be outputs of the scenario planning exercise that are used in further analysis (planning, options appraisal or scientific modelling).

Berkhout recommends that scenarios are kept simple to make them accessible and to use them with non-specialist audiences. However, in longer or more intensive scenario planning exercises, users may want to introduce surprises and feedback mechanisms. There are several ways of achieving this:

- Two scenarios can be combined (e.g. one for local or national level and one for the international level). This process needs to be selective because there are many possible combinations.

- Major shocks or extreme events are not part of the scenario storylines presented here. They can, however, be introduced during the planning process. This involves the identification of relevant "side swipes" (e.g. by means of a brainstorming session) and subsequent analysis of impacts under each scenario (see Section III.6).

- Another approach would be to introduce a third dimension (driver of change) relevant to the sector: high or low technology scenarios have been tried in a number of exercises including the Special Report on Emissions Scenarios for the Intergovernmental Panel on Climate Change (IPCC, 2000). In this case, the effects of different assumptions about the adoption of energy technologies in the future was analysed in detail for one of four socio-economic scenarios.

- If the original set of scenarios is thought to oversimplify trends, it is possible to add a second round of scenario elaboration en-couraging participants to think about feedback mechanisms. This allows learning processes to be taken into account. One option would be to organize this round of the evaluation as a "game-playing" simulation, (see Section III.8).

The stages of a project

The 12 stages of a scenarios project are described and illustrated, from identifying the focal issue or decision through decisions and/ or publicizing the scenarios. A good overall guide to the first part of the process, developing the scenarios, is to be found in Peter Schwartz's The Art of the Long View *(Schwartz, 1997). The sub-section "Getting the process right" is reproduced from Berkhout (2001) with permission of Crown Copyright.*

GETTING THE PROCESS RIGHT

Maximizing the learning benefits of scenario planning exercises requires close attention to process. Careful planning and structuring of the scenario elaboration, synthesis and evaluation stages of scenario planning are needed. The details of the process will be tailored to the needs and resources available in each case. The process needs to accommodate integration of a diversity of view-points and technical expertise, producing an iterative process combining creative, participative workshops and work carried out by individuals or in small groups to synthesize and elaborate scenarios. Realism is needed about the time and resources needed to complete an exercise – this tends to be underestimated. Time is needed in the participative aspects of elaboration and in the process of making sense of the results. Finally, stakeholders need to be involved in the elaboration of scenarios at an early stage.

The process used in the *Digital Futures* study (Wilsdon, 2001) included the following steps:

- background scoping research;

- stakeholder workshop;

- small expert group meetings;

- individual elaboration of scenarios with contribution from experts;

- presentation/consultation with stakeholders;

- final scenarios;

- input into research and policy recommendations.

The scenario elaboration workshop is perhaps the most critical stage. Key points to consider are:

- It takes time to familiarize participants with future thinking; the initial workshop should be at least a full day.

- A typical structure for the workshop might be: aim of the process, introduction to the scenario approach, presentation of scenarios, elaboration of sectoral scenarios (e.g. transport in 2020) in breakout groups, feedback, planning next steps.

- Moderation by a professional with scenario experience is recommended.

Berkhout recommends that three principles be applied in scenario elaboration and evaluation: symmetry, balance and triangulation. By symmetry, he means that equivalent effort is devoted to elaboration of all the scenarios chosen. By balance, he means that the scenario storylines and indicators should be developed as neutrally and dispassionately as possible – covering the same domains and seeking to avoid bias towards or against any particular scenario. By triangulation, he means a process of ensuring that the distinctiveness and coherence of scenarios is retained (mainly by viewing the narratives side by side).

THE 12 STEPS

Checklist for developing scenarios
This checklist extends that in *The Art of the Long View* (mentioned in the summary):

Step 1   Identify focal issue or decision

Step 2   Key forces in the local environment

Step 3   Driving forces

Step 4   Rank by importance and uncertainty

Step 5   Selecting the scenario logics

Step 6   Fleshing out the scenarios

Step 7   Implications for strategy

Step 8   Selection of leading indicators and signposts

Step 9   Feed the scenarios back to those consulted

Step 10   Discuss the strategic options

Step 11   Agree the implementation plan

Step 12   Publicize the scenarios.

STEP 1   IDENTIFY FOCAL ISSUE OR DECISION

The focal issue or decision may be obvious. For Texaco, the challenge set out by the CEO was *"What are the long-term **structural** options for Texaco's participation and **leadership** in the **energy** industry?"*, which led to a focus on three focal issues:

- that access to and ownership of exploration and producing opportunities may be constrained by the politics of the host countries and actions of the US government;

- that new intruders may get between Texaco and its customers, taking away its marketing margins and leaving the traditional industry with the commodity part of the business; and

- that environmental pressures and technological change may converge with changing social values and lead to major shifts in the mix of fuels used to produce energy in all forms.

In other cases, it needs to be teased out. For instance, for Caledonian Paper, external "Remarkable people" were used to identify the focal issue of *What is the future of paper in an electronic media world?*

STEP 2   KEY FORCES IN THE LOCAL ENVIRONMENT

Forces in the local environment will influence the success or failure of decisions about the key question. These will include customers, suppliers, competitors and internal groups. What will the decision makers want to know before they decide?

Listing these key factors is Step 2; they are sometimes referred to as microeconomic forces, and are often the factors elicited by interviews or issues workshops (see Section III.4 and the case study on Turkey [Section IV.1]).

STEP 3   DRIVING FORCES

Forces in the macroenvironment that will affect the key factors are known as the driving forces. These will include the PEST set (political, economic, social, technological), but may be extended by particular forces such as demographics or public opinion.

Research is usually needed to find the relevant drivers, and to understand their trends and possible or likely breaks in trends. Examples might be in demographics, the effect of immigration on numbers and education level of people in London, where instead of the forecast of a declining and ageing population instead a growing young population was uncovered in the *London in 2020* project (Ringland, 1998).

STEP 4   RANK BY IMPORTANCE AND UNCERTAINTY

The key factors or microeconomic forces, and the driving or macro-economic forces, are ranked on the basis of two criteria: importance to the decision identified and uncertainty.

The point, as Peter Schwartz says (Schwartz, 1992), "is to identify the two or three factors that are most important and most uncertain." These will provide the main differentiators of the scenarios, but there may be two stages before the two or three are identified.

First, some macroforces may best be felt and measured through their effect on key factors, and so are subsumed in these.

Second, do not lose sight of the fact that important but predict-able forces may be more significant to the decision than the un-certainties. This was true in the computer industry in the early 1990s, when swings to desktop machines decimated margins for traditional suppliers and dominated the race for survival (Ringland, 1997).

STEP 5   SELECTING THE SCENARIO LOGICS

The logics are the axes of uncertainty arising from the ranking. Two or three driving forces or key factors (usually driving forces) are used to create a visual map of the scenarios. The aim is to end up with a few scenarios that will be perceptively different to the decision makers.

So, for instance, if one driving force is "social values", the poles of this axis might be "individually dominated" and the other "community/consensus dominated". If the other driving force was globalization, the axis might go from "regional/local decision making" to "global forces dominate". Four scenarios could then be:

- individual/local;

- individual/global;

- community/local;

- community/global.

This raw positioning will become more complex as other factors in the scenario are added, a storyline developed and a timeline added.

STEP 6   FLESHING OUT THE SCENARIOS

Once the logics are fixed, return to the lists of driving forces and key factors identified above. Sometimes, the logics are reasonably correlated with the driving forces. For instance in the example above, a strong regulatory regime could exist in different forms according to the local/global orientation, but would not be found under a highly individually oriented society. Other factors may be constant across the emerging scenarios; for instance, technology developments might be a common factor whereas technology adoption could be argued to be higher under individually oriented societies, except where government initiatives exist.

The forces and factors need to be turned into a narrative, answering questions such as:

- How would we get from here to there?

- What events would need to happen for this to come true?

- What sort of people would characterize the scenario?

STEP 7   IMPLICATIONS

Now, the test of it all. How does the question to be decided look under the different scenarios? Do we come to the same answer under all of the scenarios? Does the same strategy fit whichever scenario plays out? For instance, in car distribution, some scenarios represented cars as commodity items, others as lifestyle choices, and their distribution could be via car showrooms or the Internet (see Section IV.3). Some of the implications for car dealers are robust across all the scenarios (e.g. develop customer links since manual aspects of servicing cannot be done over the Internet). But, for the car manufacturers, the only reasonable strategy is to work hard on developing early warning of changes in the marketplace.

STEP 8   SELECTION OF LEADING INDICATORS
AND SIGNPOSTS

It is important to be able to track which scenario is nearest to history as it unfolds. The way to do this is by identifying some events or economic indicators that would only be found as part of one of the scenarios. It is best if these can be indicators which are tracked anyway by competitive intelligence, be unambiguous (e.g. named people, companies or levels of statistical indicators). It is also important that the escalation route is clear, so that the unit that observes the trigger event knows what to do about it. An example was given in Section I.5, about the Information Society.

STEP 9   FEED THE SCENARIOS BACK TO
THOSE CONSULTED

The emphasis is on finding the right method of feedback: packaging, naming and storyline are, as in any communication exercise, vital. One-on-one feedback is preferable to groups, and applying it to a decision that the interviewee had mentioned or has by now started to face is the most effective way. For instance, using the scenarios to help solve the problem of prioritizing investments will quickly provide credibility (just follow the money).

STEP 10   GENERATE AND DISCUSS THE OPTIONS

Section III.7 describes the method of generating and deciding on options, by creating a matrix of a complete set of options against the scenarios, and grading them from very positive through to very negative. So, for instance, in an e-commerce scenario, investing in electronic channels to market would be positive, whereas the same option could be negative in a scenario focusing on traditional outlets.

The choice of options will depend on organizational capability. Most will need to follow options that span realistic scenarios, and watch for early indicators on others. However organizations that are large enough to influence the market may take a higher risk profile.

STEP 11   AGREE THE IMPLEMENTATION PLAN

There will usually be a project owner who can agree the implementation plan. This will need to cover:

● early indicators, responsibility and escalation route;

● implementation of agreed strategies and options;

● publication of/publicity for the scenarios.

STEP 12   PUBLICIZE THE SCENARIOS

Within a corporate or departmental environment, publicity methods are usually traditional – maybe a short video, slide sets, reports.

When scenarios are intended to influence public opinion or to facilitate discussion within a company, a marketing plan is needed:

- What are the target audiences?

- Who are the decision makers and who is an influencer?

- Who will benefit and who will lose out under each scenario? How can their needs be met?

- What channel can be used to reach the target audiences?

- What events are critical in time sequence?

- What are the success criteria (i.e. when do we stop!)?

Getting started

This section prompts us to ensure that the project is well-thought out. It discusses communicating the aims, scope and timescale of the project to the budget holder, setting up the team and connecting it into the organization.

HOW TO GET STARTED?

Start with a definite event: a presentation, a brief or a lunch. What to cover should include:

- the aims of the project, scope and timescale;

- the team and its reporting structure.

PRE-PLANNING CHECKLIST

Like any successful project, scenario planning needs clarity at the outset.

Aims of the project, scope and timescale
See Section III.1 on the aims and scope.

Timescale
- One-day workshops can enable a management team to plan their actions based on existing scenarios. This is easier if there are only

two scenarios (if this is the only workshop planned, introduce with the brief on the aims of the workshop and project).

- Scenario workshops taking two days can build outline scenarios that bring out the main issues in the competitive environment and initiate wide-ranging action.

- In two weeks, an experienced team with a good database of environmental analysis and intelligence can create scenarios and use them with a management team to develop new strategies.

- Six months is a more normal elapsed time to produce well-rounded scenarios and an action plan that takes the need to organize input and feedback into account, as well as to develop strategy.

- Even if the use of scenarios is seen by the team as ongoing, each stage (e.g. production of the first scenarios) will need to be defined.

- When are the deliverables required (e.g. aligned to the planning cycle, availability of key people).

What are the deliverables?
What form of output is required and to whom: in the immediate term, reporting during the project needs to be agreed. The list in Section III.8 is a guide on the type of scenario presentation for dissemination onward to the organization.

THE TEAM AND ORGANIZATION

Who is the client?
This was discussed in Section III.1.

Team
- Scenarios can be developed by one person, but they are improved by access to experienced "friends".

- A range of backgrounds is useful, including a non-public sector background.

- A core team of three is frequently chosen, and they should share interviews and workshop facilitation, preferably working in pairs. The key roles are:

    o team leader to set the overall aims and schedule who, with a network including the planners and the Board, is responsible to the project owner for delivery;

    o organization "old hand" with a wide network of people across, but especially at the front end of, the organization (e.g. project managers, call-centre managers);

    o visionary and/or outsider who is willing to pose difficult questions and comparisons.

- Other skills:

    o access to an experienced scenario planner, who may be from outside the organization, either as a consultant or taking over the delivery responsibility part of the team leader role;

    o access to a good communicator to help test output, who may well be external, and provide a neutral communication role rather than being expert in the domain or organization;

    o access to libraries or web data sources – see "Deciding the question" (Section III.4) for a discussion on the role of research, and "Linking scenarios into the organization" (Section III.8) on the role of intelligence.

ORGANIZATION

But, even more importantly, you will need links into the organization: not everything will be appropriate for all organizations or for all projects:

- The senior decision makers. How will you keep them informed, interact on the ideas as they emerge or get early wins through implementing plans based on the scenarios?:
  - ○ Advisory Board;
  - ○ progress reports to/meetings with CEO;
  - ○ work directly with the Board in workshop mode.

- The organization's middle managers and old hands:
  - ○ electronic links, Intranet;
  - ○ find the opinion leaders for and against changes;
  - ○ a low-key workshop early on with a business unit to develop all or part of the scenarios.

- The organization and industry's movers and shakers, visionaries:
  - ○ make them allies early on;
  - ○ informally discuss the ideas with them and quote them liberally;
  - ○ a workshop early on with a team built round one or more visionary.

Linking the project into the organization
- Via head of planning or senior sponsor:
  - ○ head of planning if a centrally driven project;
  - ○ senior sponsor if particular to a business unit.

- Advisory Board or "champions":
  - ○ geography and diaries may make email and online discussion forums more effective than an Advisory Board;
  - ○ champions should be forward-looking and need not be senior, but need to be role models and not frustrated with the organization.

- Mixture of workshops or interviews to get input:
  - two-day workshops give good momentum, more ideas, generate interest;
  - interviews by phone less good than face to face;
  - workshops can tackle aspects of the problem space with experts;
  - workshops can tackle "what is the question" with a mix of attendees;
  - getting the Board for two days is not usually an option.

- CEO – briefed if not involved through Advisory Board:
  - an early interviewee;
  - get suggestions for champions and interviewees/workshop attendees.

- Who to interview:
  - 100 interviews are too many;
  - 10 are too few;
  - need for a mix of line and staff;
  - need for a mix of insiders and outsiders (e.g recent hires or customers/stakeholders, partners or competitors);
  - people outside the organization who have provocative views;
  - the list will increase as you explore the questions.

- Whether to seek wider input:
  - electronic via email or Intranet, good safety belt;
  - if using volunteers for workshops, get those with time to spare rather than those with significant roles or views;

○ research and business intelligence undertaken by the organization in the context of the scenarios helps widen awareness of the project (see Section III.4 and Section III.8).

• Feedback after the scenarios are in place:

○ board or management group (in person if possible) and discuss applications of the scenarios to strategy at the same session;

○ planning group or planners across the organization (in person if possible) and discuss default scenarios in the "official future";

○ interviewees (by email or phone) unless specifically requested to visit;

○ workshop attendees (similarly by email or phone).

• Communication of scenarios:

○ team member in person usually needed;

○ slide set and/or video;

○ storyline description, with implications for organization spelled out;

○ possibly, a brochure;

○ possibly, briefing via Intranet or for public policy using a website set up for the purpose.

• First use of scenarios:

○ sponsored by board member;

○ solving a problem or developing a strategy;

○ dry run the methodology to use in advance with the team;

○ also plan for issues workshops with several management teams or groups of stakeholders.

What is the best mixture of central and dispersed activities?

- The team needs to be able to meet, for the sort of interactions that are less effective electronically.

- Interactive bulletin boards or email discussion groups can replace or augment some interviews and workshops.

- Secondees from across the organization are very valuable, as are workshops held outside the home base.

Deciding the question

This section outlines the role of research and interviews in deciding the focal question, and provides sample checklists for exposing the driving forces for some of the main applications of scenarios in business.

INTERVIEWS, WORKSHOPS AND RESEARCH

Scenarios explore the possible answers to questions about the future. They are most useful when the scenarios directly explore questions of concern to the organization. Interviews, either with individuals or groups, are usually used to create a list of factors that will affect the world and to identify the big questions. Workshops may be used to explore the factors (e.g. to get depth of understanding on a specialist area). And research will usually be needed to tie down data and known or predicted factors.

RESEARCH

Research will often involve two stages. At the first stage, research concentrates on ideas (see, e.g., Section I.2). This will identify some of the major forces affecting the organization.

Then it will usually be necessary to tie data and known or predicted factors down. However, research should always be done in the context of a specific set of questions: the gathering of data is enormously facilitated by the web, making quantitative data and qualitative data easily available. It is easy to drown the crucial areas in data and issues: teams of two are better at monitoring focus than a solitary worker. Data sources which are widely used across a range of industries and countries include:

- OECD data on developed countries;

- Economist Intelligence Unit reports;

- forecasts such as in Pearson (1998);

- industry- or field-specific analyst and think-tank reports (e.g. on health, financial services, technology);

- government statistics on demographics and lifestyles.

However, be careful of using extrapolations based on historic data: for instance, the official projections were that the population of London would decrease and age from 1990 to 2000 as it had done over previous decades; but changes in immigration, mobility of students and increases in education and media industries in London meant that by 2000 the population was younger and higher than in 1990.

SEVEN QUESTIONS FOR THE FUTURE

Most people have an understanding of how their world works, but often it is not voiced or shared. This questioning technique works on the basis that people know a great deal, but do not always know what they know.

These questions (Table III.4.1) are to trigger thinking: the key is to understand the person's perceptions and unlock their strategic thinking. The technique could be used on an organization, a company, an industry or even a country. It should be done for a specific area of interest and over a relevant timescale. They are widely used and originate in Shell.

Table III.4.1	The vital issues (the Oracle)

1. *Critical issues.* Would you identify what you see as the critical issues for the future? (When the conversation slows, continue with the comment. Suppose I had full foreknowledge of the outcome as a genuine clairvoyant, what else would you wish to know?)

2. *A favourable outcome.* If things went well, being optimistic but realistic, talk about what you would see as a desirable outcome.

3. *An unfavourable outcome.* As the converse, if things went wrong, what factors would you worry about?

4. *Where culture will need to change.* Looking at internal systems, how might these need to be changed to help bring about the desired outcome?

5. *Lessons from past successes and failures.* Looking back, what would you identify as the significant events which have produced the current situation?

6. *Decisions, which have to be faced.* Looking forward, what would you see as the priority actions which should be carried out soon?

7. *If you were responsible (the "Epitaph" question).* If all constraints were removed and you could direct what is done, what more would you wish to include?

TAILORING THE QUESTIONS

Depending on the nature of the problem to be addressed, later interviews and issues workshops may tackle different aspects and need different preparation. Some of the common questions facing business are:

- technology rate of change or adoption;

- globalization vs. regional/localization;

- commoditization vs. niche supplier;

- community values vs. individual values.

The four checklists below augment these for different classes of strategic challenge.

Political and economic change
The interviews and workshops should focus on:

- capturing the areas of fear, uncertainty and doubt;

- Creating scenarios that tackle different views of how these areas play out;

- looping back to individuals early on with outlines to ensure the real issues are being discussed.

Industry restructuring
Corporate planners and staff people may have different sets of assumptions from the views of employees on the ground. Using existing scenarios, provoke discussion about likely scenarios and the implications for the organization in:

- workshops for corporate planners – the custodians of the official future;

- workshops for business units at the sharp end that are facing change.

Flesh out the official future from planning guidelines and describe it as a scenario, then use an externally-defined scenario and compare the differences (e.g. using the list of questions above). However, the team should have done some preliminary thinking about:

- problems facing not only the competition but also the organization?;

- new sources of competition;

- success criteria of existing partnerships.

Workshops will produce more creative thinking than interviews in this environment. The key questions and opportunities will be difficult to tease out, and internal issues will take a lot of time to be set aside: SWOTs of existing and potential competition and partners are good diagnostic tools once the scenarios are in place.

New products, markets or competition
Knowledge of trends and discussion of them may be the decider in prioritizing new initiatives, rather than the differences between scenarios. However, scenarios can tackle questions like: "Who would want this?" Scenarios could also put forward different answers and timescales for each scenario.

Use the list of questions in Table III.4.1 with at least three of the leading protagonists of each view of the answer, then analyse their underlying assumptions and build scenarios to illustrate the different sets of assumptions (e.g. on the common four uncertainties). Explore their default scenario:

- initially separate groups for each initiative;

- once a set of scenarios are in place, cross-initiative workshops will bring out the advantages and disadvantages of each initiative;

- some organizations will prefer investments that are good bets under all scenarios, others may adopt an "official future" and take action accordingly.

Portfolio management
By adopting existing scenarios for the industry of the organization, the axes are likely to reflect the differences between business units particularly in relation to the common four uncertainties. Businesses that take differing views on any of these make for more difficult management, especially those that span a range of metrics and cultures.

Deciding "the question" from a set of interviews and workshops

- Define a set of terms that cover the standard areas of uncertainty; for example:

  - rate of change or adoption of technology;

  - globalization vs. regional/localization;

  - commoditization vs. niche supplier;

  - community values vs. individual values.

- Analyse the interviews using these headings and then add other categories defined as broadly as possible; for example:

  - competition;

  - staff;

  - infrastructure.

The differences in views on the topics will flavour the scenarios:

- Identify the focal issue or key decision to be made:

  - the issue may be external but the decision is about what to do in the organization;

  - the decision outcome will likely be different under different scenarios.

Interviews and workshops

This section provides guidelines and sample agendas for interviews and workshops, and discusses some tools to assist and improve the process. It notes that while interviews have been the basis of much scenario fact and issue gathering, workshops/focus groups and email/bulletin boards are increasingly being used to fit with the pace of the time, used in addition to or replacing interviews. This section has been greatly improved by thoughts from a presentation given by Adrian Davies of St Andrews Management Institute, UK.

PRACTICAL TIPS ON THE INTERVIEW PROCESS

- Consider the number of interviews carefully. Aim to get a range of views from different parts of the organization, different countries, a mixture of senior board members or in the public sector, establishment figures and identified high flyers or thinkers. Try to include people from outside the organization. The volume of information generated from these interviews made the analysis very time consuming: allow at least two hours per interview for analysis. Remember that the interview schedule will need to be extended as the project progresses.

- Plan how best to feed the "internal" issues back. Much of the information concerns internal organization and culture. This needs to be packaged and fed into the relevant areas in the organization, so that interviewees know that these ideas are not lost.

- Confidentiality. To get the best ideas and thoughts from people, it is advisable to stress that individual comments will not be attributed. Some people are nervous about taping of the interviews, and ask for assurances on the security of storage of the tapes and the control of identification of the source of each script. A scribe is useful if tapes are not being used, so that eye contact and concentration is maintained. Interviews are written up (but not usually sent to the respondent), and are kept securely by the team.

- Setting the scene. Advise the respondents before the interview that no pre-work is required. Ideally, it is best to get people away from their desk and in a different environment, so they can think creatively. In practice, the interview will be slotted into a busy senior managers schedule. In order to get people in the mood to think about the future and express their ideas, the interview needs to be relaxed and enjoyable. Most people find they jump around from one topic to another. It is best to try and encourage them, rather than make the interview seem like a set of questions with right or wrong answers.

- Set the time horizon clearly (e.g. 10 years or 20 years) and the scope (e.g. the future of information technology or the future of Scotland), and define the objectives of the exercise and anticipated output. Discuss any concerns with the timescale or scope that the interviewee might have.

- Interviews should only be constrained by the schedule of the respondent – up to say two hours. Interviewers should avoid leading questions, using, instead, the seven questions in Table III.4.1, for instance.

- At the end of the interview, the interviewer should ask whether the respondent has anything to add, and whether they had found the interview useful themselves. Leave the interviewee good time to think about both of these. Describe to the interviewee what will happen next and what will be visible to him/her.

- Plan group interviews outside the offices to encourage divergent thinking. Group interviews are not focus groups, the participants set the agenda. They are useful in, for example, country scenarios to bring in large numbers of disparate views. They usually result in consensus views, but using Groupware software (see Section III.5) can help ideas rather than personalities to dominate.

- Group and individual interviews are merged to create a "trial agenda" around a few major themes. This often reveals gaps in the evidence leading to desk research or additional interviews. The trial agenda becomes "the agenda" when a complete set is collected and collated in a formal document under change control.

ISSUES WORKSHOPS

After about 10 interviews, a few factors or issues are likely to emerge as the list of major questions to be addressed by the scenarios. All members of the team must sign them off before any issues workshops are held. The list should be fed back to the CEO or client, as should any unwelcome items in the evidence.

One way of testing that these are the right issues, how they interact with each other and how they may change over the timescale of the scenarios, is to enlist the help of a group of challenging people (interviewees and outsiders) to create an outline structure. The issues should be considered in the order:

- External world:
  - issues already raised;
  - what else is important?;
  - what are the interactions?;
  - when are they most important (now, later).

151

- Interface to customers, markets, competition (this is often the section where most new thinking arises in groups):
  - issues already raised;
  - what else is important?;
  - what are the interactions?;
  - when are they most important (now, later)?;
  - changes in barriers to entry or exit;
  - new players.

- Internal factors:
  - issues already raised;
  - what else is important?;
  - what are the interactions?;
  - when are they most important (now, later)?;
  - part of organization to follow up.

Use memorable quotes from the interviews to enliven the issues workshops, and, at the end of the issues workshops, any options for strategy that have emerged should be captured for evaluation.

SCENARIO-CREATION WORKSHOPS

The agenda in Table III.5.1 works well for management teams. For disparate groups, who do not share assumptions, a longer timescale may be required. Global Business Network organize scenario workshops that take a week. It is best if the workshop is residential, to allow extra discussion time: at the very least, it must be off-site.

The scenario workshop should involve the whole team and be limited to the team. After the workshop, the scenarios should be written up by one person, who also identifies trigger or branch points between scenarios. In writing scenarios, speculation and evidence-based elements need to be distinguished.

Table III.5.1   Agenda for a two-day workshop

Day 1:

a.m.: meet, introductions

- questions for the Oracle
- review process to be followed (see Section III.2)
- brainstorm factors

p.m.:

- separate out the likely givens from the trends and uncertainties (see Section III.6); mapping all the issues captured to date on a predictability/uncertainty vs. importance matrix
- cluster the uncertainties into building blocks – maybe four or five
- decide on the interesting combinations; choose from two to four as scenarios

Day 2:

a.m.:

- review the combinations
- write a scenario story for each chosen combination

p.m.:

- describe an evolution sequence for each
- look for turning points
- review Oracle questions
- discuss the implications.

WORKSHOPS BASED ON EXISTING SCENARIOS

Working with business units and basing the workshop on existing scenarios (Section III.1) allows the team to:

- familiarize themselves with scenario thinking;

- work with views of the future;

- extend the scenarios to describe the impact on their own business;

- develop a set of plans based on the scenarios.

An agenda is given in Table III.5.2.

Table III.5.2 Agenda for a one-day workshop	
Aim:	Develop strategy for organization
	• Envisage the futures
	• Brainstorm the changes
	• Plan development programme
Attendees:	Functional group, management team, planning team
Pre-reading:	Scenarios
Duration:	$2 \times \frac{1}{2}$ days or one day
First module:	• Briefing on scenarios
	• Brainstorm: events and trends specific to the business or function
	• Build list of services for 2005 (syndicates for each scenario)
	• Report back
Second module:	• Assess for each service or market: effect of trends and scenarios, size of market, key skills, core/ bought in
	• Report back from syndicates
	• Five top opportunities
	• Report back
	• Action planning

TOOLS FOR USE IN WORKSHOPS

Using tools can significantly improve the results of planning events or activities by:

- increasing the number of ideas generated;

- increasing communication between individuals and groups;

- increasing the clarity of common understanding;

- increasing the resilience and coherence of the scenarios.

There is a good discussion in Azim (2000).
　　Traditionally, flip charts and overhead foils have been used: even the simple step of replacing these with capture on word-processed documents, which can be communicated using email, often carries significant dividends.
　　During the building of scenarios, tools come in at several stages:

- generating ideas;

- capturing ideas and finding common content;

- grouping the ideas and factors into themes;

- sorting the ideas and factors into trends and uncertainties;

- testing the logic with influence diagrams.

Generating ideas
With groups that have not been exposed to scenario thinking before, it can increase the comfort factor if a groupware tool is used to generate and display ideas. One such tool is Ventana, details on http://www.ventana.com

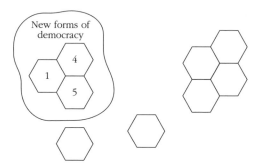

Figure III.5.1   Clustering.

Capturing ideas and finding common content

Tools can reduce the time needed to analyse interview data. One which is used by the sizeable research group at the University of St Andrews is the NUD*IST software package. Details are on http://www.qsr.com.au

Grouping the ideas

One widely used method of grouping ideas (Figure III.5.1) uses IDON's hexagons. These are about six inches across, and can be written on with felt tip pens – and wiped clean to make changes. Each member of the group contributes as many ideas and factors on hexagons (one per hexagon). These are then grouped with discussion into similar ideas or themes, which will form the building blocks of the scenarios (Galt et al., 1997). IDON (now trading as Metabridge) also provide software to aid in the documentation of workshop discussions and outputs. More detail can be found on http://www.idongroup.com

Sorting into trends and uncertainties

The standard tool used to sort ideas and factors is the two-dimensional matrix shown in Figure III.5.2. Group discussion in workshop mode is an essential aspect of this step. It develops a consensus on the trends – the forces or changes which are relatively well expected – and the uncertainties.

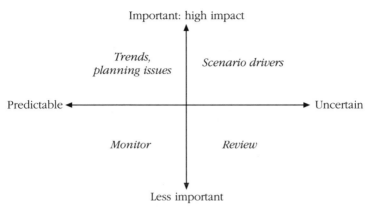

Figure III.5.2 Trends and uncertainties.

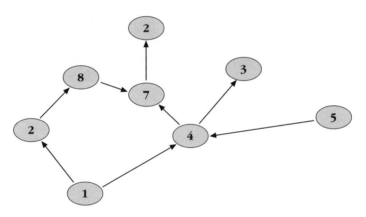

Figure III.5.3 Influencing diagram.

Influence diagrams

These are important for identifying the driving forces and testing the logic of the scenarios (an example is shown in Figure III.5.3). A tool that allows a group cooperatively to create a logic flow system is Decision Explorer: details can be found on http://www.banxia.com

Scenario creation

This section describes building a basic set of scenarios, and ensuring that they are believable and coherent. Creation of story-lines and characters take different skills from the analysis stage of scenario building. It is also important to decide how many scenarios are needed and the relative importance of external and internal factors. The subsection "Taking account of major shocks" is from Berkhout (2001) and published by permission of Crown Copyright. The classification of "Types of Scenario" is based on ideas from Dr Alexander Fink.

STRUCTURING THE IDEAS

This is one of the most important steps in creating a common vocabulary and understanding. So, in the case studies "Foresight into insight" (Section IV.6), "Healthcare 2010" (Section IV.7), "Preparing for a new energy environment at Statoil" (Section IV.2) and "Reframing industry boundaries" (Section IV.4), this step was done with as wide a group as possible. One of the ways to do this is via an influence diagram, which shows what contributes causally to what factor. An example, using the development of violence and social unrest, is shown in Figure III.6.1 (from van der Heijden, 1996). Other groups use the hexagons discussed in "Interviews and workshops" (Section III.5). Ways more suited to expert teams are discussed in 'From data to scenarios" (Section I.3) and "New car distribution" (Section IV.3).

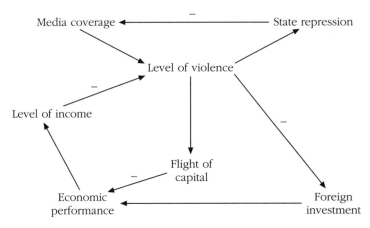

Figure III.6.1 Starting an Influence Diagram (van der Heijden, 1996; reproduced by permission of John Wiley & Sons, Ltd).

TYPES OF SCENARIO

How scenarios are used in strategic planning and management depends on the organization's possibility of influencing the occurrences described in the scenarios. Alexander Fink from ScMI distinguishes three different types of scenario.

External scenarios
External scenarios exclusively consist of external influences that cannot be controlled by the organization. A manufacturer of automatic tellers, for example, could intend to use such scenarios to consider the development of the market over the next 15 years in order to draw conclusions about product planning. External scenarios put complex boundary conditions, that cannot be significantly influenced by the organization, into the centre of attention.

Internal scenarios
Internal scenarios only take factors under the control of the organization into consideration. For example, the product features of an automatic teller machine are decided on by the manufacturer. With

159

the help of internal scenarios, new product concepts or business models can be elaborated.

System scenarios

System scenarios are a mixed form of external and internal scenarios. Here, the scenario field contains external environmental influences as well as internal guidance dimensions. In this case, the scenario field presents the complete system of decision field and environment. System scenarios have to be handled with special care because they contain environmental conditions as well as action options.

The selection of a suitable scenario scope (i.e. the determination of an external, internal or system scenario) mainly depends on the market power of the organization and the strength of the relevant external influences. Smaller organizations can be compared to sailboats that are carried in certain directions depending on weather and current. They mostly concentrate on external scenarios in order to derive decision options for their own course.

However, organizations with major market power can be compared to ocean liners that often make decisions independent of the swell of the oceans. This is why they often work with internal or system scenarios.

BUILDING THE SCENARIOS

The first step is sorting into trends and uncertainties, usually on a whiteboard at a scenario workshop. Discussion among workshop members is crucial at this stage, and using the "Trends and uncertainties" matrix in Figure III.5.2 is the usual method.

The trends are pulled out as common to all scenarios (e.g. demographics). The important uncertainties are grouped, using Post-it notes, hexagons or influence diagrams, until a few – up to four are manageable – big ideas are visible and agreed on, and posed as a question (e.g. will competition be dominated by global players or not?).

Table III.6.1 Coral Reef and Deep Sea scenarios				
	Individual values?	*Innovation*	*Open cultures?*	*Less government?*
Coral Reef	Yes	Yes	Yes	Yes
	Yes	Yes	Yes	No
	Yes	Yes	No	No
	Yes	Yes	No	Yes
etc.				
Deep Sea	No	No	No	No

Then a matrix is developed, with the big ideas along the top, and values shown as "yes" or "no". Each combination is given a name, and the interesting combinations to be followed up as scenarios – by developing a storyline – are agreed. Part of the matrix for the *Coral Reef* and *Deep Sea* scenarios discussed in Part I was as shown in Table III.6.1. In this case, the scenarios were chosen to be very coherent to simplify their adoption.

HOW MANY SCENARIOS? AND WHAT TYPES?

Four/three/two? More?
Generally, more than four is too many for the differences to be clear and useful – but there are exceptions. The list below identifies strategies for choosing the number and type of scenario and looks at target audiences:

● Four scenarios encourage divergent thinking and are useful for creating vision:

  ○ difficult to maintain clarity of separation;

  ○ often the consequence of two-dimensional thinking (e.g. orthogonal axes and population of each quadrant);

161

o one quadrant often not viable, though it may be the desired world for a business;

o four scenarios may be chosen to represent "visionary", "business as usual", a difficult scenario and a benign environment.

- Three scenarios lead to the expectation that one is "the forecast":

  o in engineering-led organizations, often a belief that "the middle one" is the best estimate;

  o based on high/low growth interpretation of scenarios;

  o not so applicable when scenarios are qualitatively different.

- Two scenarios allow two very distinct (not necessarily "low" or "bad" vs. "good" or "high") scenarios to be developed:

  o comparatively easy to communicate;

  o best for mass use in building common language;

  o one version may be "official future" or default scenario vs. visionary scenario.

- It may be that the data used to create future worlds give natural groupings that lead to a specific number of scenarios. All of these can be used to consider options for action, though they may be grouped later (Section IV.3, "New car distribution").

- If there are several competing technologies, each may define a different scenario for "how the world might be" and then there would be as many scenarios as technologies, as in the KRONE case study in Ringland (1997).

- Consider choosing scenarios to include one "surprise-free" scenario based on existing trends, an "ideal" future for the organization (normative scenario) or worst-case fears about the future.

Target audience

- Experts developing new strategies:
  - as many scenarios as fit the main competing underlying technologies, policies or geographies;
  - each technology, policy or geography is treated as a different world;
  - normally, the number of scenarios gets reduced after preliminary analysis.

- Planners:
  - two if detailed modelling of each scenario is planned;
  - four if trying to explore a new competitive environment, major changes in culture, etc.;
  - often professionally interested in exploring underlying assumptions and connections.

- CEO and Board:
  - two scenarios to ensure that the two-minute synopsis (the elevator speech) can capture the essence of the difference between the two worlds;
  - possibly three if a Board workshop is planned to examine the implications of the scenarios for corporate strategy;
  - four are usually lethal;
  - mostly interested in early indicators or predictors and what to do next about a specific current issue.

- Middle managers and business unit managers:
  - as for Board and CEO.

- Mass communication:
  - two for clarity;

○ four if all four are equally of interest;

○ all scenarios communicated must be compelling and different visually and qualitatively.

DEVELOPING THE STORYLINE

The storyline that expresses the scenario needs to communicate the important aspects of the scenario, being in addition provocative, memorable and vivid. At the same time:

- A story needs to have a beginning (maybe in the past), a middle (maybe the near future) and an end (e.g. at the end of the scenario timescale).

- The story needs to be anchored in the past and leading to hypothetical events in the future. Using prototypical characters is often helpful: What sort of people would dominate in each scenario and which lose out?

- The logic of each scenario needs to be capturable in a simple diagram, allowing it to be understood as a whole. This underpins "the elevator speech" which is the 30-second description covering all the scenarios.

- The differences between the scenarios should be clear, and names are an important part of aligning them to different worlds.

- Internal consistency is improved by using influence diagrams to see the causal connections between events.

- A sequence of events should populate the storyline in time sequence, expressed in terms that relate to observables (e.g. "UK joins the European common currency", not "UK pulls closer to Europe").

- A small set of elements are defined for all the scenarios, and their different values or outcomes are described for each (e.g. in one scenario "Mergers and acquisitions increase" and in another scenario "Mergers and acquisitions decrease and companies spin components off or break up").

- Key variables should be quantified and early indicators listed. Early indicators should be events or variables tracked by the organization, unless they are very short term and can be checked by a specific piece of research.

STORYLINES FOR SPECIAL PURPOSES

- In organizations that are not experienced in scenario thinking, it can be helpful to write a "surprise-free" scenario, representing the official future of the organization. This may flesh out the fact that different parts of the organization are operating under different assumptions.

- Phantom scenarios can be developed to explore the logical outcomes of particular sets of assumptions held in the organization, as a way of testing their validity.

TAKING ACCOUNT OF MAJOR SHOCKS

The exploratory and synthetic approach used in these scenarios suggests that change occurs gradually along a single trajectory. Future states are seen as being the outcome of an accumulation of changes over time that all point in the same direction. But not all change is like this. The direction of change may itself vary over time, with one set of conditions being replaced by a new set. This change in direction may take place slowly (as part of the process of economic and social development), or it may happen suddenly as a result of major, surprise external events (such as terrorist attacks or rapid changes in the natural environment). If the change is slow it may be possible for one scenario to be superseded by another (e.g.

a shift from *Coral Reef* to *Deep Sea*). If the change is sudden, the question to be asked is how "resilient" a given scenario is to its impact. Answering this question will be very difficult, mainly because large-scale, unanticipated events are hard to foresee. Berkhout suggests that governments and other organizations build up inventories of "shock" events, by scanning conventional and unconventional sources and through brainstorming. The question of resilience could then be investigated by applying the shock to each of the scenarios and trying to assess how easily each of them could recover or adapt to their impacts.

Scenarios to plans

This section discusses making decisions about what to do based on scenarios, and provides a set of matrixes to help the analysis and decision process depending on the risk profile of the organization. It is based on the methodology used by ScMI as described by Dr Alexander Fink, and is reproduced by permission of ScMI.

INTRODUCTION

One of the ways in which scenarios are used is to support decision processes in strategic planning.

On the one hand, this can relate to the evaluation of alternatives. This could be, for example, in regard to proposed capital projects or competing product development projects, or the evaluation of existing strategies or strategy variants. The evaluation of pre-existing decisions and strategies is a *passive scenario transfer* (i.e. one or more of the action options that are examined with the help of scenarios already exist). In this case, opportunities and risks related to every aspect within the individual scenarios have to be considered. The scenarios become "testing environments" for strategies and decisions. On the other hand, scenarios can be used for the creation of new strategies at any level in the organization and across functional areas. The updating and creation of strategies is an *active scenario transfer.* The stages of scenario-supported strategic planning are shown in Figure III.7.1. This section concentrates on Stage 3 of this process, "Strategy finding", and on 4(c), "Strategic positions".

167

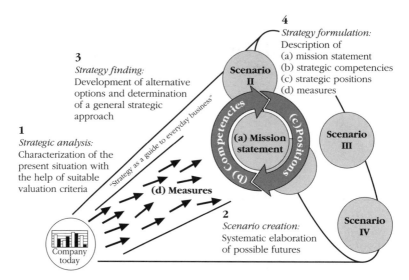

Figure III.7.1   The four stages of strategy (reproduced by permission of ScMI).

STRATEGIC ANALYSIS

Strategic analysis is the first step. It describes the current situation with the help of suitable methods and tools – using well-known instruments of strategic planning like portfolio analysis, critical success factors, PIMS or SWOT analysis, or business segmentation.

SCENARIO CREATION

The second stage, *scenario creation*, describes possible future developments affecting the organization. By proceeding systematically, even decision situations of high complexity and uncertainty can be included and made manageable for the next step.

STRATEGY FINDING

The central step in creating new plans is *strategy finding*. First, review the opportunities, threats and their related options for action that have been determined in the different scenarios. Here, the rule of thumb is to keep all scenarios "in the game for as long as possible". This way the opportunities and (often suppressed) risks of a superficially viewed "good" development, occurring in a mostly negative scenario, can be determined. Similarly, there may be a mixture of opportunities and threats in scenarios that are regarded as positive. At the end, planners and managers of the scenario project have to decide if the strategy should be built on one or on more than one of the scenarios. If the strategy is based on a selected reference scenario, it is called "strongly focused". A "future-robust plan" is based on several scenarios.

Focused planning can serve two functions: The reference scenario can be the basis of a focused strategy that presents the final result of strategy development. Alternatively, contingent strategies can be developed. These are complete strategies, which describe how an organization could act optimally if a certain scenario occurred. So the decisive question is: "What shall we do if a certain scenario comes true?" and not: "What will happen?" Afterwards, the contingent strategies are included in robust planning.

AN EXAMPLE

Figure III.7.2 shows the *strategy finding* step of a scenario project for a medium-sized manufacturer of industrial semi-finished goods (i.e. supplier to trade). Four external scenarios have been created. Specific action options have been elaborated and summed up. The scenario options matrix shows whether the determined options were only suitable for Scenario I or whether they were also valid under other scenarios. Using options that are positive under several scenarios gives a future-robust core of strategy, giving the planners the certainty: "We are relatively safe in using these measures".

Consideration of the options led to identification of a partly robust strategy for Scenarios I, II and III. These options, together with the core of strategy, now described the strategic orientation of the organization. But, because it was not possible to completely rule out Scenario IV, two further steps were necessary. First, a contingent strategy was elaborated for Scenario IV. Then, early

169

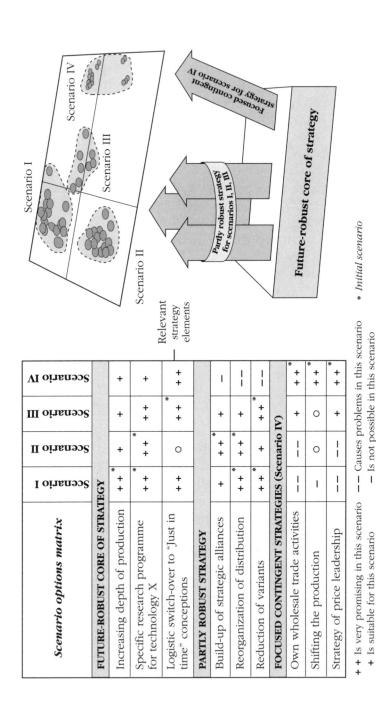

Scenario options matrix	Scenario I	Scenario II	Scenario III	Scenario IV
FUTURE-ROBUST CORE OF STRATEGY				
Increasing depth of production	+ + *	+	+	+
Specific research programme for technology X	+ + *	+ + *	+ +	+
Logistic switch-over to "just in time" conceptions	+ +	O	+ + *	+ +
PARTLY ROBUST STRATEGY				
Build-up of strategic alliances	+	+ + *	+	–
Reorganization of distribution	+ + *	+ + *	+	– –
Reduction of variants	+ + *	+	+ + *	– –
FOCUSED CONTINGENT STRATEGIES (Scenario IV)				
Own wholesale trade activities	– –	– –	+	+ + *
Shifting the production	–	O	O	+ + *
Strategy of price leadership	– –	– –	+	+ + *

+ + Is very promising in this scenario   – – Causes problems in this scenario   * *Initial scenario*

+ Is suitable for this scenario   – Is not possible in this scenario

O Is neutral in this scenario

Figure III.7.2 Scenario options matrix (reproduced by permission of ScMI).

indicators were identified which drew attention to tendencies of the environment towards Scenario IV. The organization has to watch these indicators closely. Should the situation develop correspondingly, the organization has the possibility rapidly and flexibly to change to the contingent strategy – "Plan B".

STRATEGY FORMULATION

The process of *strategy formulation* (Step 4) starts once the strategic orientation has been settled. Recurring parts of company and business strategies are mission statements, strategic competencies and strategic positions as well as concrete measures. The important thing about this is to see the mission statements as "big outlines that make the blood surge through the veins". A mission statement is put in concrete forms by the use of strategic competencies ("What do we have to have or be able to do in order to achieve our mission statement?") and strategic positions ("Where do we have to offer what to achieve our mission statement?"). The concrete measures finally build the bridge between the present and the objectives described in the mission statement, competencies and positions.

FIVE FORMS OF STRATEGIC POSITION

In choosing a strategic position, two factors are important. One is the ability of the organization to influence the competitive environment. The other is the organization's attitude to risk, in terms of choosing a focused or a future-robust planning style. Five typical forms of scenario-supported strategic positioning follow (Figure III.7.3).

1. React to recognizable trends
Here, the organization orients its planning around the scenario with the "highest probability". This requires the basic agreement of the persons involved about the most probable occurring future. The advantage of this over traditional planning is that it relies on a

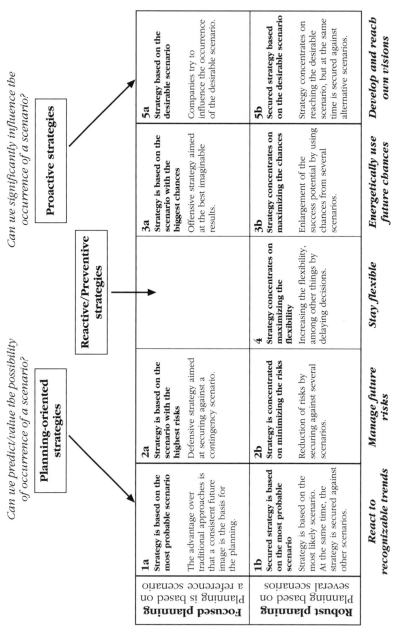

Figure III.73 Strategic positioning (reproduced by permission of ScMI).

consistent future image that has been developed "in competition" with possible alternatives, as distinct from a default scenario often based on past experience. A focused strategy based on the most probable scenario can be supplemented by being secured against the occurrence of other, less probable scenarios. It is also possible to identify decision points in which a "transfer to another scenario" is planned.

2. Manage future risks

An organization can minimize its risk by building its strategy on the basis of the scenario that presents most threats to the organization. Specific forms of this variant are contingency strategies or contingency plans. For the development of a contingency strategy, a very extensive and coherent contingency scenario is needed, normally a system scenario including internal and external factors. An organization can also try to minimize the risks altogether by choosing a future-robust strategy based on the occurrence of all the worst threats. The problem with this approach is that it may well cause the planners to ignore opportunities. More productive is the use of threatening scenarios to actively manage the risks to the organization.

3. Energetically use future chances

An organization can build its strategy on the scenario with the biggest upside potential given by the environment. This approach is quite promising but also very risky because it ignores less promising scenarios. At the same time, it should be considered if there are possibilities to bundle several strategies into one aggressive strategy related to positive factors in the competitive environment.

4. Stay flexible

An organization becomes more flexible by gearing its strategy to several scenarios and making some specific decisions dependent on the occurrence of events or early indicators from individual scenarios. This is often combined with an operating plan based on a robust core of assumptions or factors that are common to several or even all scenarios. This combination does, however, increase the danger of putting strategically important decisions off.

5. Develop and reach own visions

An organization can also try to influence the occurrence of desirable scenarios. This kind of proactive planning mainly occurs in internal scenarios and strongly controllable system scenarios dominated by key factors that can be influenced. In this case, focused strategy development means to decide on one scenario and to use the resources of the organization following a strategy to implement it. This has two risks. If the scenario turns out to be strongly influenced by external environmental factors, it may be hard to change direction if they change. Second, an organization can become overextended if it tries to implement plans fitting several scenarios at once, while a competitor completely focuses on a single scenario that, in the end, really occurs.

A proactive approach based on a desirable scenario can be supplemented by additionally securing the strategy against other scenarios. This especially makes sense when scenarios contain significant environmental influences.

TWO COMMON ERRORS IN USING SCENARIOS

Adopting one external scenario

Organizations often develop several external scenarios at great expense. But strategic planners get discouraged at the thought of really thinking through the implications of multiple futures. Often, pressure from top managers to express planning situations in simple decision models contributes to this. So, the planners settle on one external scenario too quickly and let the success of the strategies they develop be dependent on the occurrence of this particular scenario.

Getting bogged down with alternative action options

Another mistake is made by organizations that develop and present action options in the form of internal scenarios and try to follow all of the action options at the same time. This way of proceeding violates the strategic principle of the concentration of power. In this case, competitors who just follow one direction and who consequently use their resources for the acquisition of capability to follow this direction will have an advantage.

SECTION III.8

Linking scenarios into the organization

Dissemination of scenarios is crucial for ensuring implementation of ensuing strategies. This section discusses dissemination tools and the use of business intelligence and war gaming as ways of increasing linkage. It includes ideas from an article by Kent B. Potter of Bennion-Robertson Incorporated in Atlanta, Georgia, USA (Potter, 2001), and is published with the permission of Risk Management Bulletin. *For more information contact* kent@bennion-robertson. com.

INTRODUCTION

This section focuses on two aspects of linking into the organization referred to but not covered by previous sections:

- dissemination to the target audience;

- links to the intelligence gathering and analysis of the organization.

DISSEMINATION

What does a scenario look like?
Draft scenarios will be presented to the project team and various working groups to resilience-test them and explore the implications. Systems diagrams may be used to explore the

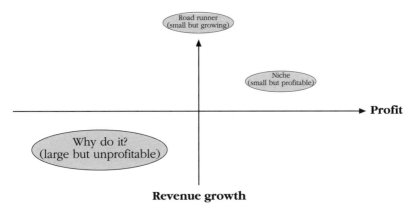

Figure III.8.1 Perceptual map.

interdependencies of factors and often provoke discussions about the underlying assumptions. However, they are probably more an analysis than a communication tool.

The most usual way of exposing scenarios back to the team or to immediate collaborators is via some sort of perceptual map. This shows the named scenarios on a 2 × 2 matrix and may give extra information (e.g. by varying the size of the bubbles representing revenue, as in Figure III.8.1).

Final scenarios
The final scenarios will need to be disseminated to several audiences:

- In tabular form, for planners expecting to rerun the current operational plan against the scenarios. But good scenarios may well not share some of the assumptions built into the plan. Many organizations believe that the best use of scenarios is before getting to this level of detail.

- To the Board, in slide set form plus a written report. The key slide will often be a set of recommendations.

- More widely in the organization, using a slide set plus a brochure containing illustrations and examples of the scenarios and their implications for strategy, (see Section IV.1 "Turkey").

- Printed storyline, for wide distribution in the organization, covering, for instance:

  o a view of the political world in this scenario;

  o the economic forces;

  o social structures;

  o the role of technology;

  o winners and losers, heroes and role models;

  o early indicators of each scenario.

- Very widely in the organization, as part of discussion/decision groups (see Section IV.6, "Foresight into insight" and Section IV.7 "Healthcare 2010"):

  o mock newspapers, films or CD-ROMs for initiating workshops on the implications of the scenarios, for instance;

  o short, five to ten minutes of film;

  o actors to play scenario vignettes are also successful.

LINKS TO INTELLIGENCE

Scenarios will live in an organization if people use them in their day-to-day work. One particularly important area is aligning the research and intelligence-gathering operation of the organization to watch emerging trends or discontinuities flagged by the scenarios. While traditional ongoing research will undoubtedly play a part, early indicators are oriented towards specific events which can be tracked through intelligence.

What distinguishes intelligence from other research?

- Intelligence is normally "entity focused", meaning that it tends to focus on named players in the marketplace, not on mass or generalized trends. This means that intelligence is well suited to help convert observations about generalized trends into clear data about specific emerging threats or opportunities.

- Intelligence is normally predictive, or future focused, although often with only the near-term future in mind.

Scenarios and Intelligence

Scenarios are most useful to the organization when they are integrated into the organization's operation; for example:

- successful at aligning leaders with a future vision for long enough to change direction;

- used to help rank-and-file employees change internal cultures to meet emerging or future external requirements;

- used to help planners who are already well connected with the changing environment.

An intelligence approach and toolkit can contribute to these aims:

- discussion about key intelligence topics picks up where scenarios dialogue leaves off, helping planners move from considerations of the future to early indicators (see Section III.2) and contingency planning (war games also offer considerable help here);

- a systematic approach to intelligence gathering aligned with the scenarios helps middle and lower echelons align themselves with the future vision by actively contributing to a future-looking, externally-oriented strategy;

179

- disciplined intelligence gathering as part of an ongoing system for collecting external information helps better ground each round of scenario planning.

The Thread of Intelligence

During the scenario process, intelligence has a different role at each phase (see Figure III.8.2):

1. At early stages, the organization may define broad, exploratory scenarios that identify major drivers and key trends, but not yet the entities that will operate within them. During this phase, research can contribute to the investigation of long-term trends.

2. It may be possible to identify emerging players and to flesh out scenarios within which those players have a role. This may also start to happen naturally over time. This is the juncture at which key intelligence topics should be more crisply defined and assessment models built. War gaming can also begin to be effective at this juncture, to examine different strategies.

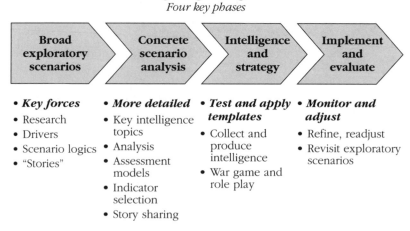

Integrating intelligence
Four key phases

Broad exploratory scenarios	Concrete scenario analysis	Intelligence and strategy	Implement and evaluate
• *Key forces*	• *More detailed*	• *Test and apply templates*	• *Monitor and adjust*
• Research	• Key intelligence topics	• Collect and produce intelligence	• Refine, readjust
• Drivers	• Analysis		• Revisit exploratory scenarios
• Scenario logics	• Assessment models	• War game and role play	
• "Stories"	• Indicator selection		
	• Story sharing		

Figure III.8.2 Integrating intelligence (reproduced by permission of *Risk Management Bulletin*).

3. As time progresses, entities that were only dimly visualized "over the horizon" during the first two steps begin to emerge more clearly. This is where more traditional intelligence collection and analysis, and fully fledged war gaming, can be very effective.

4. Strategies that emerged during the initial scenario-building processes (first two steps) and are completely defined during the third step, are fully implemented and evaluated. As part of this evaluation, planners wisely loop back to Step 1 and consider broad, exploratory scenarios to examine what "else" might be coming over the horizon in terms of emerging opportunities and threats.

This is shown schematically in Figure III.8.2.

Main points

The aim of this part has been to provide a set of checklists to help managers plan and implement successful projects using scenarios. There are cross-references to the case studies throughout the checklists, which should help recall of the origin of the checklist item or guideline.

SCENARIOS ARE PART OF STRATEGIC MANAGEMENT

Any use of scenarios must relate into the organization for:

- rationale – why scenarios are desirable;

- budget, timescale, outputs;

- framework for implementing actions based on outputs.

SCENARIO PROCESS

The process described applies to projects where the need is for:

- output for use by management to help their decision making;

- creation of vision in an organization, leading to strategic decisions;

- strengthening of a management team by creating a common language.

THE USE OF SCENARIOS RATHER THAN THEIR EXISTENCE IS THE SIGNIFICANT FACTOR

- It may be possible to use existing scenarios to achieve the goals.

- Using scenarios throughout an organization to improve decisions requires focus on dissemination tools and techniques.

- Simple scenarios may achieve as much or more than complex ones, depending on the target audience and desired outcome.

PART IV

CASE STUDIES

SUMMARY

This part of the book contains a number of case studies chosen to illustrate the range of applications of scenario thinking. They span the four major challenges facing organizations – the political and economic environment, industry restructuring, tackling new markets, and managing a portfolio. They also span a range of industries – from forestry to high tech – and a range of project timescales and techniques.

POLITICAL AND ECONOMIC ENVIRONMENT

"Preparing for a new environment of energy at Statoil" (Section IV.2) and "A study in Turkey" (Section IV.1) focus on the political and economic environment for business. The Statoil project has evolved over several years, while the Turkish project reported within a few weeks.

The Statoil scenarios concentrated on the economic impact of new patterns of energy consumption, and found that the "unthinkable" scenario would become very apparent within two years. In Turkey, questions were about political directions and possible instability: the study was used to re-examine the company's strategy in the country.

Both projects used qualitative techniques for creating scenarios: in addition, the Statoil project used causal loop thinking taken from System Dynamics to explore the stability of scenarios.

185

INDUSTRY RESTRUCTURING

New competition and industry restructuring were the concerns that drove the scenario projects "New car distribution of the future", "Reframing industry boundaries" and "Software for collaborative working". The range of industries concerned with industry restructuring – covering the software industry from car distribution to forestry and paper making – is indicative of the sweeping changes being encountered and anticipated.

The case study on "New car distribution" used a formal method of creating many potential scenarios and, by clustering, derives fewer "final" scenarios. The "Reframing industry boundaries" case study explicitly used the scenario process to create understanding between two companies with interdependence. The software case study was chosen to show how companies can develop competitive strategies internally. In each case, the main benefit seen was the recognition of emerging competitors or changes in the industry, providing a framework for initiating action.

NEW MARKETS

The focus behind the work at Texaco over four years was to find new market opportunities as the future unrolls. While many parts of the project used standard scenario-creation techniques, the case study focuses on their revision and evolution as they were used in the company. In the case of the health-care markets, investigated by Glaxo over a year, the focus was to determine whether and how to enter the new diagnostics market. Both projects found that scenarios provided an analytic basis for recommendations to the CEO: in the case of Texaco by identifying the challenges and proposing responses, at Glaxo by creating a synthetic future from elements of the scenarios as a basis for action.

PORTFOLIO OF BUSINESSES

A trading group in the City of London used scenarios in a short workshop to explore the tacit assumptions of the management team and their application to the Group's portfolio of businesses. Although the scenarios used were of *London in 2020,* the underlying assumptions proved relevant to decisions much more immediately.

A study in Turkey

This project for a multinational group was facilitated by Adam Scott and Adrian Davies of St Andrews Management Institute, as part of a set of ongoing projects by the group to review manufacturing and marketing strategy. The case study was written by Adam Scott and Adrian Davies and is reproduced with their permission.

BACKGROUND

The taxi driver at Istanbul Airport gave us an immediate choice between the scenic drive around old Constantinople, with its Byzantine city walls and historic and magnificent places of worship, or the speedier drive on new roads where the taxi's own speed seemed only to be exceeded by the rate at which the meter tallied up Turkish lira in their hundreds of thousands. Turkey's fascinating situation was summed up by an impasse between a shiny black BMW and a shiny new Mercedes in a narrow old street near our hotel.

In Turkey, Europe meets Asia, the Black Sea flows into the Mediterranean and ancient trade routes have adapted successfully to a modern world. Turkey is Islamic, and in all public buildings Atatürk's portrait looks down with a stern and watchful eye on every development as it has for some 80 years. Some differences between Atatürk's Kemalism and Islam are summarized in Figure IV.1.1.

At the time of our study in 1997, the Welfare Party, an Islamic group, held sway in the secular republic with the sufferance of the Army and of the Constitutional Court. Erbakan's Welfare Party, with just 21 per cent of the popular vote, was ruling in a fragile coalition with Mrs Tansu Çiller's True Path Party, which had 20 per cent

Pillars of Islam	Arrows of Kemalism
I. Creed	☐. Populism
I. Prayer	☐. Republicanism
I. Fasting	☐. Nationalism
I. Charity	☐. Secularism
I. Pilgrimage	☐. Statism
I. Struggle in the way of good	☐. Reformism
Medina provided a model Muslim community and Islamic law is known as the *shari'ah* dating back to 600 years after Christ.	The doctrine of Mustapha Kemal Atatürk, founder of the Republic of Turkey in the wake of the Ottoman Empire and winning the war with Greece 1919–1922. He died in 1938.

Figure IV.1.1 Islam and Kemalism (reproduced by permission of Adam Scott and Adrian Davies).

support. Rampant inflation took the attention away from a vibrant economy, most of which is unrecorded despite being overwhelmingly evident on the ground.

Behind democratic government in Turkey stood the National Security Council, which had just informed the government of the need to take "a number of anti-fundamentalist measures" (*Turkish Daily News*, 13 March 1997). Indeed, the Army was said to have encapsulated its views in twelve conditions that emphasized the secular nature of Turkey's democracy. These included respect for Atatürk, education of secular-minded and constructive citizens, and religion as a spiritual experience but not as the foundation of the state. The Army portrayed itself as being identified with society and defending democracy internally, just as it defended the country externally.

THE QUESTIONS FACING THE CLIENT

1. *What would the impact of changes in the political, social, cultural and religious environment in Turkey be on their business?*

2. *What particular signals would provide warning signs?*

In particular, the client was concerned about potential change in the influence of Islamic political philosophy and practice and how this change might require their business to adopt different approaches to its local operations whether in trading or in manufacturing. If Turkey were to develop a stable and distinctively Islamic civil society for the 21st century, what might that society look like?

CONDUCTING THE STUDY

Collating the initial data

We started with desk work, reading up readily available material and networking to establish a suitable list of contacts and potential interviewees.

Apart from desk research and discussions with local staff, we conducted 18 interviews, mostly one on one but some involving the client's project leader as an interviewer in addition to members of the team from St Andrews. More than half the interviewees were Turkish, and we sought out individuals who were well informed about Turkey with academic (four persons), business (seven including two employed within the client group), journalistic (four) as well as political (one) and government/diplomatic (two) backgrounds. We conducted some preliminary work in the UK and then 12 of the 18 interviews in Turkey were conducted over a four-day visit, though some flowed into the three-day visit for the issues workshop and a second three-day visit for the scenarios workshop.

We complemented the interviews and workshops with working lunches with senior politicians and leaders of the Turkish equivalent of the Confederation of British Industry. The statements made during the interviews were transcribed using Microsoft Word, coded, sorted and edited into a 62-page workbook for the issues that the workshop was scheduled to cover. At this stage, it was also possible to provide a "natural agenda" and to appreciate some of the gaps in our plan that would prove difficult to fill in the given timescale.

Reviewing the input data

We realized that there were limitations to the political input that we had received, in terms of the range of opinions, levels of society and the geographical spread: we had not been out into the regions of Turkey and we suspected that we were receiving elitist views and insufficient insights into the Kurdish question. To a small extent, this was offset by less formal conversations with individuals, but we had not met a broad cross section of Turkish society.

Islam was clearly a constant theme in Turkish culture and society, however secular the Republic that had been constituted by Atatürk. For most Turks we met, their religion was a relatively low key and private faith as Atatürk had intended. However, in the streets, there was evidence of younger people more publicly fervent in their faith and, for some, faith was guiding political thinking and significant welfare action at a local level in urban communities. Young Turks seemed to be ultra-sensitive to any criticism of their country.

Turkey, already a NATO member, found itself in an intriguing geographic location. It was right in the middle, between Europe and the Middle East, and yet strangely isolated: drawn in many ways westwards into the Council of Europe, aspiring to membership of the European Union (having had earlier promises) and developing a modern industrialized economy with great potential for tourism, and yet often finding itself rejected, in tension with Greece, not least over Cyprus and criticized for its record on political corruption, on its handling of the Kurds and on human rights. Turkey had not aligned itself against the modern state of Israel, and, while we were engaged in our study, the Chiefs of Staff of the two countries were meeting.

It was not difficult for critics of the West to find ammunition and to suggest that Turkey needed values grounded in Islam, in traditions that went back beyond Atatürk and into developing its own distinctive culture. Such ideas could find breeding grounds among students and intellectuals, among the more traditional urban middle classes and among recent migrants into the cities.

Segmenting the population
We considered how to segment the population in terms of income and lifestyle and identified:

Western-oriented "super-elite"	0.2 million
New rich and educated second generation	0.5 million

Middle class (living like a "Danish" middle class)	5.5 million
Aspiring to be middle class	5.0 million
Subtotal of "modernizing" Turks	*11.2 million*
New urban – growing at up to 5 per cent per annum	25.0 million
Rural balance	26.4 million
Sub total of "traditional" Turks	*51.4 million*
Overall total	*62.6 million*
1997 forecast for 2005 with growth having peaked	80.0 million

This gave us an underpinning for designing the issues workshop (see Section III.5).

The issues workshop

Normally, we map issues between importance and uncertainty and then consider influenceability, but, on this occasion, we were also considering the ability of the client to cope with a variety of outcomes. Since the participants had not worked together before, and the scope was wide, we allowed 48 hours (see Figure IV.1.2).

Issues Workshop timetable and topics

Tuesday afternoon
- An overview of Turkey

Tuesday evening
- Social and demographic developments and trends

Wednesday morning
- Politics

Wednesday afternoon
- Politics moving into economics
- Macroeconomics
- Microeconomics

Wednesday evening
- Diplomatic – Turkey in the world, in the Turkic community and relating to neighbours, to NATO and to the EU

Thursday morning
- Local politics and attitudes
- The environment
- The principle threats
- The position of Turkish consumers

Figure IV.1.2 Issues workshop timetable and topics (reproduced by permission of Adam Scott and Adrian Davies).

The balance of internal and external forces	Internal	External
Positive	• Robust microeconomics • Ability to muddle through macroeconomically • Stable democracy • The Army as a source of stability	• Continuing US support • Trade relations with the EU • Trade with Russia, Central Asia and the Middle East • Strategic location geographically
Negative	• Kurdish problem • Reform of the Kemalist legacy • Creeping Islamicization of institutions • Social conditions in the cities • Quality of political leadership and players • Rent seeking is entrenched	• Turkish "PR" (human rights, child labour, drug smuggling, . . .) • Water politics in the region • Greece – a range of issues • Shift in EU attitudes • Image with other Islamic regimes

Figure IV.1.3 Forces on Turkey (reproduced by permission of Adam Scott and Adrian Davies).

We also mapped the forces that appeared to be acting on or within Turkey (Figures IV.1.2 and IV.1.3). We also considered the range of options in the light of forces for change (Figure IV.1.4).

THE SCENARIO SPACE

We developed two axes for picturing our scenarios outside an unreformed Kemalism. The grey area in Figure IV.1.5 delineates the space in which the forces shaping Turkey's future were battling for dominance.

One possibility was that Turkey would remain within the central

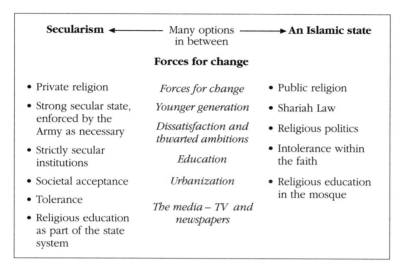

Secularism ←——— Many options ———→ **An Islamic state**
in between

Forces for change

• Private religion	*Forces for change*	• Public religion
• Strong secular state, enforced by the Army as necessary	*Younger generation*	• Shariah Law
	Dissatisfaction and thwarted ambitions	• Religious politics
• Strictly secular institutions	*Education*	• Intolerance within the faith
• Societal acceptance	*Urbanization*	• Religious education in the mosque
• Tolerance	*The media – TV and newspapers*	
• Religious education as part of the state system		

Figure IV.1.4 Forces for change (reproduced by permission of Adam Scott and Adrian Davies).

	Tolerant	Reformist	
	Democratic	Rational	
	Unreformed Kemalism		
		Lifestyle flexibility	
Isolated			Western
Rejected	**Respect for diversity**		Integrated
	Less tolerant	Populist	

Figure IV.1.5 Scenario space (reproduced by permission of Adam Scott and Adrian Davies).

space. Threat of military intervention, intervention by the President or Constitutional Court, or reaction to right-wing Western European attitudes might all have kept Turkey there. This was called "Unreformed Kemalism".

195

To move "North-east" required politicians to adopt a social justice agenda, with military support for a developing civic society with centre-party democracy and, in due course, full EU membership.

If Islamic politicians had become electorally much more successful with increasing pressure from their clientele to become more radically Islamic – heading "South-west" – then it seemed likely that the Army would move in to restore a "North-eastward" movement.

Another possibility was a combination of increasingly nationalistic (but secular) politics, with absolute rejection by the EU of Turkey's application for membership.

THE SCENARIOS

We called the "North-west" corner the *Turkic corner*, the "South-west" we named *Islamic experiments* and the "North-east" was *Charismatic technocracy*. If Charismatic technocracy eventuated, Turkey would increasingly resemble any other South-east European country.

We prepared detailed scenarios around the main political characteristics; these scenarios have been summarized and simplified in the following subsections.

1 The base position – variations on a theme – Unreformed Kemalism

Government would alternate between different moderate coalitions and would be guided by the Army, with the intention of avoiding formal confrontations and intervention by the President. In parliament, opposition would not be coordinated or effective. The media would find that existing limits on their freedom of expression were tightened.

The Turkish economy would remain fragile and corrupt. At the time of the study, Turkey kept postponing a meeting with the IMF; that formal meeting with the IMF would continue to be postponed with macroeconomic management drifting, ongoing public-sector deficits, high real interest rates and around 80 per cent inflation. Although both the political and macroeconomic situations would appear fragile, microeconomic growth and associated corruption would continue.

On the diplomatic side, with domestic political machinations continuing to rumble on, less than effective attention would be paid to issues like the relationship with the EU and the future of Cyprus.

Looking further ahead, there would be an election and Turkey might move into another scenario or muddle along with the same trends predominating until a crisis occurred.

2 Charismatic technocracy

Threshold: A new coalition emerged after Erbakan's retirement, maybe after losing a confidence motion. Some other old leaders would be thinned out, possibly with the assistance of the West, in appointing long-standing leaders to EU or UN positions.

Technocratic coalition: The Army would support a four-party coalition under a leader yet to be identified.

Macroeconomics: An early meeting with the IMF would have led to a three-year programme to deal with ongoing public-sector deficits through privatization, private finance initiatives and tax reforms.

Social justice: To guard against Islamic resurgence, the coalition would have had to act on issues of social justice and on effective delivery of social welfare.

Trade: As confidence builds up in the political and macro-economic situations, microeconomic growth would have accelerated, stimulated by private finance initiatives and the success of Turkish traders.

Diplomacy: With confidence growing, effective attention would have been paid to issues such as creating a fruitful relationship with the EU, even if Turkey had less than full membership, and making a constructive contribution to wider European problems (e.g. those in the Balkans and in Cyprus).

Outlook: A democracy with credible central parties able to lead Turkey towards a tolerant, rational, democratic future in which respect for Islam's spiritual values was combined with acceptance of up-to-date Western macroeconomic management, robust tackling of social welfare by a judicious mix of public and private-sector initiatives and microeconomic growth at a speed consistent with economic qualification for EU membership. This does not necessarily solve the religious/cultural/racial barriers to entry sustained within the EU by Western European domestic political forces.

3   Islamic experiments – populist and putting Western Integration on the back burner

Threshold: A new coalition with a suitable accommodation with Islamic politicians, concentrating on issues of social justice of concern to their electoral clientele.

Islamic experimentation: The middle class in particular would wrestle with a conflict between "Islamic values" and consumerism, but media advertising would continue.

Macroeconomics: Building discipline into macroeconomic management might *not* be a high priority, but Islamic politicians would be keen to demonstrate competence, prudence and honesty. Welfare spending could be offset by privatization and politico-social pressure to pay tax.

Trade: Microeconomic growth continues, but perhaps not as swiftly as in the "Charismatic technocracy" scenario.

Diplomacy: Less attention might be paid to creating a deeper relationship with the EU and more to the social needs of Muslim communities in the Balkans and in Cyprus. We would expect contacts between the military in Ankara and Washington, DC to reassure the US authorities that Turkey was not realigning itself.

Outlook: A realistic Islamicist pragmatic approach could, with encouragement, lead to a tolerant politics akin to that of some Christian democracies in Western Europe, but, if the route moved towards "idealistic isolationism", the Army might well intervene.

4   The Turkic corner – a stabilized distinct Turkey – pressed into a nationalist corner by EU right-wingers

Threshold: Opposition to Turkey's aspirations for full membership might have caused a deep sense of frustration and isolation throughout the senior political, military and commercial circles in Turkey.

Turkic corner: Turkey might then have turned in on herself politically and diplomatically. Internally, politicians would seek to stabilize the situation using resentment against the EU as a powerful unifying factor.

Trade: Trade, though still important, would face bureaucratic delays; trade negotiators would start the tortuous process of providing a better framework for the Black Sea Council and for better links further to the north and east.

Economic implications: Microeconomic growth could have been good by EU standards but not match Turkey's potential.

Diplomacy – Turkey's Turkic and Muslim sphere of influence and US relations: Turkey would want to play a more significant part in the Balkans and the former Soviet republics. It would have continued to look to the USA for affirmation of its role within NATO both militarily and diplomatically.

But there could be significant tensions within the Army and government caused by any number of flashpoints; for example, economic difficulties; ethnic problems in the Balkans; Greek, Kurdish or Azerian pressures; any of which could result in confrontation.

Outlook: Turkey could develop into a "new Byzantium": a self-respecting republic determined to make its own way in the world unshackled by EU bickering and mature enough to handle the challenges mentioned above without aggression.

5   The "Silent Coup"
We also envisaged what we called the *Silent Coup* or the Military Corridor back to a secular scenario. The detail was very specific to conditions at the time, and it would have involved the Army and the Constitutional Court acting in concert. This scenario has not been developed in detail.

THE STUDY OUTCOME

The final outcome of the study has been mapped (Figure IV.1.6) in a format matching that for our initial diagnosis, showing the space in which Turkey's future is being contested and four quadrants, representing the basic scenarios into which (over time) the

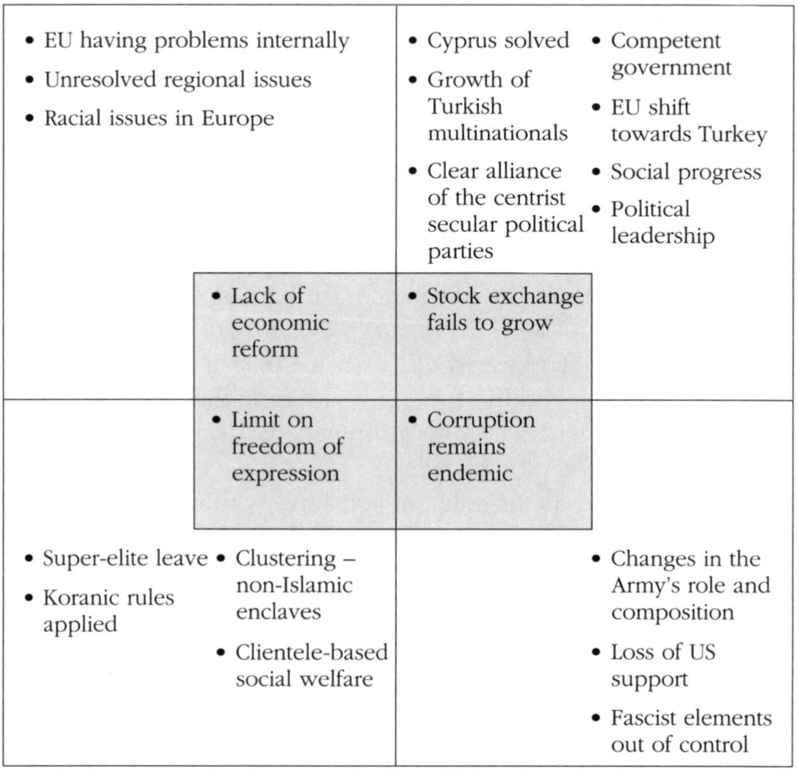

• EU having problems internally • Unresolved regional issues • Racial issues in Europe	• Cyprus solved • Growth of Turkish multinationals • Clear alliance of the centrist secular political parties	• Competent government • EU shift towards Turkey • Social progress • Political leadership
	• Lack of economic reform	• Stock exchange fails to grow
	• Limit on freedom of expression	• Corruption remains endemic
• Super-elite leave • Koranic rules applied	• Clustering – non-Islamic enclaves • Clientele-based social welfare	• Changes in the Army's role and composition • Loss of US support • Fascist elements out of control

Figure IV.1.6 The study outcome (reproduced by permission of Adam Scott and Adrian Davies).

balance of forces may drive the country. The space representing the forces on Turkey today is shown in grey, and a number of signals are identified to show the future scenario space that Turkey may move to occupy.

COMMUNICATING THE STUDY

The task of using the study within the client group lay with their project leader. The material was marshalled into a 30-page Microsoft Power Point presentation for use with an oral presentation.

WHAT HAPPENED?

Most of the forces that we observed and described are still in play in Turkey. Shortly after our study, the Welfare Party lost power and was later proscribed, as was the Virtue Party, its successor as Turkey's principal Islamic party, in June 2001. The Virtue Party had 102 of the Turkish parliament's 550 members at the time it was banned: some members were expelled but most were permitted to stay on as independents. In August 2001, a fresh attempt to create a new Islamic party was launched by an ex-mayor of Istanbul. In the same month, *The Economist* reported that Mesut Yilmaz of the secular and conservative Motherland Party believed that Turkey's "national-security syndrome" was the major obstacle to democratic reforms sought by the EU.

Turkey has endured both political and economic problems, with corruption still an issue, and international pressure for economic reform. It has continued to press for membership of the EU, though the EU has other candidates, formerly under Soviet influence, who are likely to be admitted first. Turkey's record on human rights remains a key factor inhibiting its entry to the EU.

REFLECTIONS

As usual, the study was conducted within time and resource constraints. These precluded the client company from a detailed level of involvement and also the involvement of individuals beyond the project team in the workshops. There was a greater reliance on published sources than in other scenario exercises conducted by a similar team in other country-specific studies. Nevertheless, the study gained the support of client local management for their decision making: the client business has continued to trade but has not embarked on manufacturing in Turkey.

Preparing for a new environment of energy at Statoil

This is an account of a project initiated by Hans Gjennestad of Statoil International E&P with a process and research designed and facilitated by Tony Hodgson of Metabridge. Philip Mathieu, Head of Corporate Strategy, guided the further developments, during which the "Unbelievable" scenario proved to be near the truth for this Norwegian oil company. The case study was written by Tony Hodgson and is published with his permission.

BACKGROUND

Statoil is the Norwegian oil and gas company. In 1998, a Statoil corporate strategy project team decided to look beyond the current working assumptions of their oil and gas business. A thorough review of strategy had just been completed and a position taken that looked robust for the foreseeable future. However, the planners felt that the edge of the foreseeable future was shorter than the lifespan of the strategy and it would be a good time to shift from first-horizon thinking to second-horizon thinking. In the first horizon, current strategic assumptions hold valid; in the second horizon, current assumptions need to be questioned.

The starting point was the formulation of a core question. The simplicity of the question that emerged hides the struggles needed to clarify the direction that would determine the emerging shape of the scenarios. Conversations made several turns of the spiral in parallel with the exploration of the relevant trends and uncertainties. However, the process of clarification was essential because it also provided the basis for inviting a wide spectrum of Statoil staff

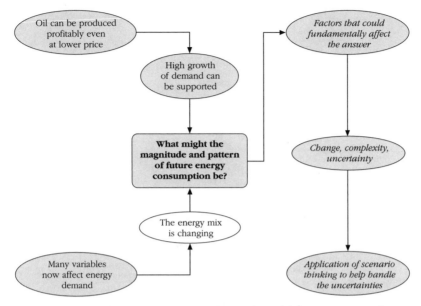

Figure IV.2.1   The Core Question (reproduced by permission of Tony Hodgson).

and executives to a scenario-creation workshop that tapped into the multiple perspectives involved in the question.

THE CORE QUESTION

The question emerged as

What might the magnitude and future pattern of energy consumption be?

The rationale that led to scenario work around the question is shown in Figure IV.2.1. The upper input to the question represents the discipline imposed by a low oil price combined with the usual forecasts of global growth. The lower input represents the emergence of an energy market closely coupled to demand, combined with an expanding energy mix. Questions about changing patterns of demand and energy mix then opened up the typical

203

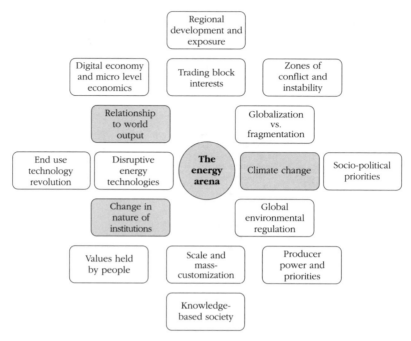

Figure IV.2.2 Factors influencing future energy patterns (reproduced by permission of Tony Hodgson).

region of trends and uncertainties, which calls for a scenario approach.

A scenario-creation workshop was organized in October 1998 with two main tasks:

- establishing the most significant trends and uncertainties;

- synthesis of an initial hypothesis of differentiated future scenarios.

To help achieve the first, a preliminary application of a de Bono CAF – Consider All Factors – (de Bono, 1985) was carried out and boiled down to a depiction of the energy arena (Figure IV.2.2). This provided a map to help knowledge elicitation to be comprehensive and not overly focused on one or two areas. Around 15 people were involved in the two-day workshop, including strategic planners, technology-futures experts, health and safety managers and external advisers. The crux of creating profound differences between scenarios is to enable a *complex of uncertainties* to be identified and considered. But this makes for great complexity. However, by applying what might be called fuzzy systems thinking facilitated by the use of hexagons (see Section III.5 and Hodgson, 1994), it is possible for a group to have deeper conversations about connectedness between factors. They then begin to see emergent patterns that are more profound than a mere checklist of factors. Groups or clusters of uncertainties that have mutual impact can then be distilled into the major bifurcation axes that will differentiate one future world from another.

The two axes that emerged from the hexagon mapping are shown in the next two diagrams (Figures IV.2.3 and IV.2.4).

The vertical axis maps the persistent uncertainty, over and above underlying trends, in the direction of sustainable development. Clearly, the issue of climate change tends to dominate this area, but there are many more factors at stake here.

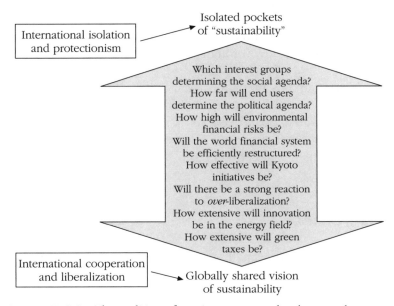

Figure IV.2.3 The politics of environment, technology and economy (reproduced by permission of Tony Hodgson).

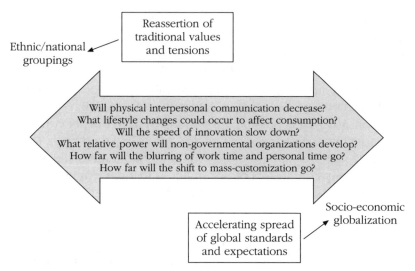

Figure IV.2.4 The future shape of consumer patterns (reproduced by permission of Tony Hodgson).

It is worth noting that since 1998 we have seen both the issues of global sustainability (e.g. the Gore/Bush battle in the USA and the struggles of the Kyoto process) and the emergence of serious anti-globalism (from Seattle through Davos to Genoa) coming into prominence.

The horizontal axis maps the persistent uncertainty around the progress of globalization of markets. Most scenarios over recent years have taken globalization as a driving force, but, even in October 1998, the Statoil scenario group was considering the counterforces that could slow or stall such progress on a number of counts.

THE SCENARIOS

The axes create four distinctly different spaces in which the future might unfold. The art here is that each combination is more than the sum of its parts. A scenario is not simply an addition of checklists of conditions but a dynamic structure that is driving the behaviour of that world and tending to sustain it in the midst of countervailing

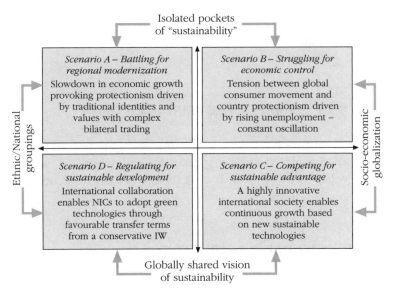

Figure IV.2.5 The four scenarios and some key distinctions (reproduced by permission of Tony Hodgson).

forces. To test and develop this, causal loop diagrams were developed for each quadrant. The gist of the story is summarized in the four boxes in Figure IV.2.5:

- *Scenario A – battling for regional modernization* – results from tension between the forces of liberalization and the forces of self-containment and isolation, combined with low concerns for sustainability.

- *Scenario B – struggling for economic control* – is a tension between a globalizing economy and eroded social conditions in Europe.

- *Scenario C – competing for sustainable advantage* – creates advantage by combining globalization with sustainable development through enterprise.

- *Scenario D – regulating for sustainable development* – combines a global shared vision of the need for sustainability with the

struggles of the international political community to accommodate their national interests.

DEVELOPMENTS AFTER THE FIRST SCENARIOS

Table IV.2.1 shows how some of the important themes in the development of the global energy market looked when the scenarios
were developed in 1998 and what transpired over the next three
years.

DIGGING INTO DEEPER STRUCTURE

To develop deeper distinctions between the scenarios, rather than
leave them as shades along the spectrum of the vertical and horizontal axes, each quadrant was investigated with the question:
What underlying systemic structure would tend to sustain the
energy world in that position? The method used was causal loop
thinking taken from the qualitative end of system dynamics. The
assumption is that any scenario that could endure for a period
would tend to have reinforcing loops[1] that propel it to grow and
balancing loops[2] that would keep it in check. The analysis is quite
complex but simplified versions are shown in Figure IV.2.6 to give
the reader a sense of how deeper structural analysis can work.

   This type of modelling can be taken to more technical lengths
through application of system dynamics computer simulation. One
of the best examples of this has been developed by John Morecroft
at the London Business School, (Morecroft and Marsh, 1997). Oil-
focused scenarios play out a dynamic between producers, oil

---

[1] A reinforcing loop is a systemic structure in which the initial cause is boosted by
the effect it creates. An example would be the growth of a population through
multiple generations of sexual reproduction – more and more rabbits.

[2] A balancing loop is one in which the greater the cause the greater the push-back
or counter-effect. An example would be the growth of predators associated with a
food population – more and more foxes that eat the rabbits. Typical reinforcing
and balancing loops tend to oscillate the overall condition of the system.

Factor	1998	2001	Actual developments	Scenario implications
OPEC and oil price	$10 a barrel with OPEC weak	$20–30 a barrel and OPEC strong	OPEC reasserted itself	Pushes towards Scenario A
Renewable energy	Merely a side show, Scenario C is not credible	Worthy of serious investigation	Emergence of economically viable wind and solar power coupled with accelerating concern over global climate change	Perhaps Scenario C is happening after all
Climate change and Kyoto	USA might ratify under Gore	Gore/Bush stalemate on the cusp followed by the Bush removal of USA from Kyoto	Kyoto struggling on Bush under fire but making continuous headway	Still in the middle of tension on the vertical axis Scenarios C and D less likely?
Globalization	Globalization is where its going with WTO getting stronger, etc.	The push back may be stronger than anyone thought	Davos protest to World Economic Forum Genoa protest to G8 London protests by anti-capitalists, etc.	On the horizontal axis, the forces are pushing harder towards fragmentation
Investment	Only token investment in renewable energy	Collapse of high-tech investment but attention turned to renewables	Rapidly increasing venture capital flows into energy technology	Scenarios C and D more likely than before
Economics of renewables	Weak economic arguments for alternatives to hydrocarbons	Increasing justification for investment in wind and solar	Wind farms increasingly common Photovoltaics on buildings	Impetus towards Scenario C

Table IV.2.1 1998 and 2001 (reproduced by permission of Tony Hodgson).

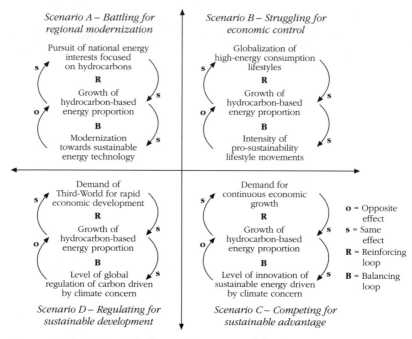

Figure IV.2.6 Simplified core dynamics of the four energy worlds (reproduced by permission of Tony Hodgson).

majors and independents. The core dynamic structure modifies as different context scenarios are superimposed. This gives, for example, a way of studying how competition works out in different scenarios.

THE IMPACT OF THE SCENARIOS

The set of scenarios has found its way into a number of applications in the strategic thinking at Statoil, as an effective challenge to conventional thinking and a stimulus for breaking new ground. The main applications to date have been:

1. *International Oil:* In the early days of the scenarios' application at Statoil, the scenario that gave the most problems was *Scenario C – Competing for sustainable advantage*. The general mindset

was that any investments around renewable energy by companies such as Shell and BP were basically reputation management, not substantial intentions towards sustainable energy. Also, it was not believed that businesses would take up renewable energy and sustainable development as a *cause majeur.* Over a period of two years, this view changed as the scenario had the desired effect of "cognitive priming" and signals began to be seen that some initiatives on renewables were breaking through underneath the hype.

2. *Oil trading:* The scenarios as they were initially developed intrigued the oil trading planners and led to a more focused exercise on the implications of the scenarios for strategy. This was especially related to the then possible partial privatization of Statoil and the possible change in the policy of the Norwegian government on state interest in oil and gas. By having four scenarios and exploring three different governmental policy outcomes, Statoil executives were able to rehearse future positions. Since June 2000, Statoil has become a partly privatized company.

3. *Renewable energy:* As part of the change from an oil and gas company towards an international energy company, the question of renewable energy came higher up the agenda. An initiative was launched to look into a broad category of "new energy". A development of the scenarios was used to provide a context for work on potentials and priorities, and the company determined which scenario was desirable and which they felt able to make happen. This is a major sea change for a corporate population reared for 25 years on the supremacy of hydrocarbons.

THE FORCES THAT ARE STILL PLAYING OUT

The set of scenarios are not forecasts. The original uncertainties are still present, albeit with new twists and turns and the emergence of new factors. Some of the main forces in tension are shown in Figure IV.2.7. For example, the "Global Compact of Nine Principles"

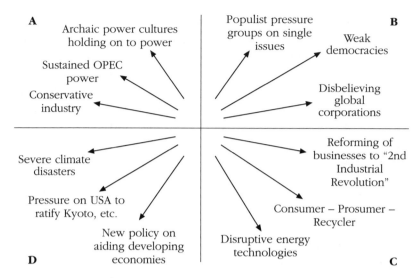

Figure IV.2.7 The energy market wars (reproduced by permission of Tony Hodgson).

initiated by Kofi Annan at the Davos meeting of world business leaders in 2000 did not exist at the start of the project. Many of the mega-mergers in the industry have happened since then. However, the socio-political issues around sustainability and globalization are more centre stage than ever and the uncertainties surrounding them even more challenging. In this sense, although these scenarios undergo constant refreshment, their fundamental relevance still holds and they still challenge new thinking on strategies of both the existing oil and gas business of Statoil and new business development.

New car distribution of the future

This case study by Alexander Fink of ScMI explores the changes in industry structure arising from changing lifestyles and the use of e-commerce to buy cars. It is published with permission of Scenario Management International AG.

BACKGROUND

The marketing and distribution of new cars is currently undergoing a radical change and posing many questions:

- Will new cars be bought via the Internet?

- Which distribution channels will automobile manufacturers choose?

- Will direct distribution or franchised dealers dominate?

- What will be the effect of mergers?

- What will the distribution outlets look like in the future?

- Can the traditional auto shop survive?

- What role will cars play in the future: rationally-chosen transport or emotionally-chosen lifestyle accessories?

- What will the competition between automobile dealers look like?

213

Against the background of these and many other questions, it becomes clear that simple answers could only present a small part of the future. The development of future-robust strategies requires the systematic illumination of future possibilities. So, ScMI cooperated with the Fraunhofer-Application-Centre for logistic-oriented business administration to outline six possible scenarios, using the internationally acknowledged methodology of Scenario Management™. The aim was to sensitize the varied groups of decision makers to possibilities and to encourage industry players to investigate possible options. The project took place in 2000 and was presented in 2001.

THREE PHASES OF SCENARIO CREATION

The process of scenario creation is based on the three-phase Scenario Management approach of ScMI shown in Figure IV.3.1.

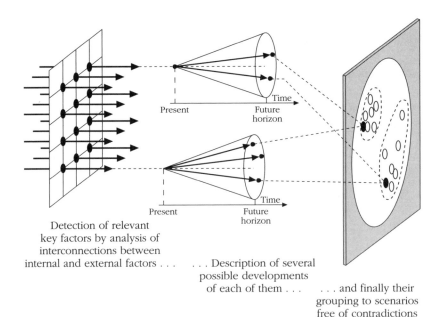

Detection of relevant
key factors by analysis of
interconnections between
internal and external factors . . .   . . . Description of several
possible developments
of each of them . . .   . . . and finally their
grouping to scenarios
free of contradictions

Figure IV.3.1 Three phases of scenario creation (reproduced by permission of ScMI).

Scenario field and key factors (Phase 1)

A scenario field – here, new car distribution of the future – is characterized by a variety of related factors. In order to consider the possible developments of this scenario field, it is necessary to identify the driving forces. To do this, the scenario field is divided up into *system levels* (business, business environment and global environment) and *influence areas* such as politics, economy, society and technology (in this case, concentrating on "Automobile Distribution" and "Customers/Markets"). Within the *influence areas*, 107 concrete *influence factors* were identified and defined. Often, an essential added value is the common definition and description of the *influence factors*. Systematic behaviour was examined by analysing the influences; for example:

- Which are the relevant leverages?

- Which factors are merely indicators of system behaviour?

- Which factors best express the system dynamics?

Then, the 18 *key influence factors* (KF) most relevant for the four influence areas for new car distribution were selected:

- *Automobile Distribution* is described by the key factors Places of Consumption/Car Shops (KF1), Incentive Systems (KF2), Use of Online Media in Distribution (KF3) and Online Providers (KF4).

- *Automobile Manufacturers* is expressed by the factors Shaping of Distribution Channels (KF5), Brand Management (KF6), Performance Spectrum of Manufacturers (KF7) and Marketing Strategies of the Manufacturers (KF8).

- *Automobile Dealers* contains the key factors Contractual Obligation to the Manufacturer (KF9), Performance Spectrum of the Dealers (KF10), Competition in Trade (KF11) and Cooperations in Trade (KF12).

- *Customers/Markets* as well as the global environment are described by the factors Significance of the Automobile (KF13), Buyer Behaviour (KF14), After-sales Support (KF15), Loyalty to Brand and Affiliated Group (KF16), Loyalty to Dealer and Trade (KF17) and Internet and Electronic Business (KF18).

Future Projections (Phase 2)

A number of development possibilities were considered for each of the key factors. This phase of scenario development is very important because the content of the scenarios – and hence the quality of decision support – results from the thorough and imaginative selection of key factors and good thinking on their evolution.

We searched for *trends* of the individual key factors and *critical dimensions* to describe future developments. They were combined into multidimensional *future projections* which can already be interpreted as "small scenarios". These projections were formulated and explained so that they could be easily and rapidly understood by persons who were not directly involved in the process. This way of proceeding is illustrated by the projections of the key factor Online Providers (KF4):

- *Manufacturers dominate Internet portals* (Projection KF4-A): Automobile manufacturers dominate Internet portals with their strong market position. Their size allows them to easily invest large amounts in portals. Internet providers supply the necessary infrastructure without being able to influence their content.

- *Dealers dominate Internet portals* (Projection KF4-B): Manufacturers miss the opportunity of adapting their distribution channels to the Internet; so, it is possible to draw information from their sites but not to purchase an automobile. The trust of purchasers is held by dealers on the ground, which enables a real as well as a virtual purchase. Because of this customer-oriented strategy, dealers dominate Internet portals.

- *Independent providers dominate Internet portals* (Projection

KF4-C): Independent Internet providers offer new cars via the Net. This facilitates a fast and uncomplicated purchase of new cars. All brands are offered in the portals and manufacturers deliver directly to the portals. Manufacturers and dealers find it even harder to keep loyal customers. Distribution via Internet portals is standardized and the manufacturers provide the necessary information. Only customers with need for personal advice turn to the dealers, and these customers expect an exclusive service.

- *Battle for the portals* (Projection KF4-D): Manufacturers, dealers and Internet providers all offer the possibility of purchasing via the Internet. Because of parallel systems, no standard can be developed for distribution over the Internet. The providers hinder each other.

Link future projections to create scenarios (Phase 3)

Once alternative future projections had been developed for all the key factors, the scenarios were then built in five steps:

1. *Check projections for inconsistency:* Scenarios are tales from the future. Their credibility is based on individual elements – here, future projections that have been developed in advance – and combinations of elements. Individual projections are paired up in a consistency matrix. Comparison of several consistency evaluations increases mutual understanding about different estimates of future developments – a significant added value of the process lies in discussions linked to refinement of different evaluations.

2. *Go through all possible combinations:* After checking individual projection pairs for consistency, the entire possible set of combinations are checked for their inconsistency: How well do the single projections match? Are there any complete inconsistencies that make nonsense of a combination? A combination is considered useful when it contains exactly one future projection for every key factor. Such a combination is called a *projection*

bundle. Analysis of *projection bundles* is a combinatory problem, which involves considerable expense if there are a great number of key factors. In this case, 7,558,272,000 imaginable combinations had to be checked. This makes the use of computers inevitable and leads to a list of consistent *projection bundles* that are most suitable to describe future scope. The list is called the *projection bundle* catalogue.

3. *Draw up a useful number of raw scenarios:* Scenarios result from grouping similar *projection bundles* together. The number of scenarios is not determined beforehand but results from a cluster analysis. The number is the result of the following compromise: on the one hand, a higher number of scenarios facilitates a very detailed view into future scope; on the other hand, planners (and later decision makers) are interested in a small number of scenarios. This helps in reducing the expense of further work on the scenarios and makes their communication much easier. The outlines of the raw scenarios come into view as the clusters emerge: How many projection bundles does a raw scenario consist of? How many times do future projections appear in the projection bundles of a raw scenario? Are there projections dominating all raw scenarios? Are there projections that are merely of peripheral importance? The answers to these questions can be found in the *scenario catalogue,* which shows the interim results of the scenario creation. In this case, a solution with six raw scenarios was chosen.

4. *Develop comprehension of individual raw scenarios:* Now, the scenario developers explore the futures characterized by the individual raw scenarios. For this, they identify those projections that are relevant for each scenario. These projections are called elements of the scenarios. Once the elements of the individual scenarios are identified, the scenario developers review all the projections again. If projections are only found in a single scenario, they are called *characteristic elements* of that particular scenario. The discussion and linking of the central elements of a scenario – above all, the characteristic

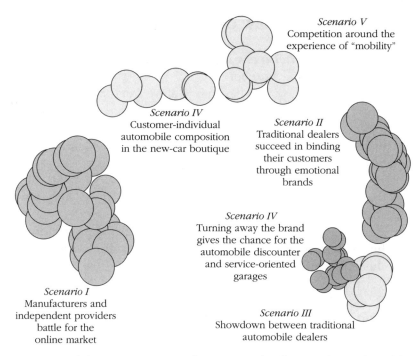

Scenario V
Competition around the
experience of "mobility"

Scenario IV
Customer-individual
automobile composition
in the new-car boutique

Scenario II
Traditional dealers
succeed in binding
their customers
through emotional
brands

Scenario IV
Turning away the brand
gives the chance for the
automobile discounter
and service-oriented
garages

Scenario I
Manufacturers and
independent providers
battle for the
online market

Scenario III
Showdown between traditional
automobile dealers

Figure IV.3.2 Six scenarios of new car distribution (reproduced by permission of ScMI).

elements – give an impression of the content and dissociation from other scenarios.

5. *Graphically present the grouping of the scenarios:* The different projection bundles are presented in a scenario mapping that places similar bundles very close together and different bundles far from each other (see Figure IV.3.2), where individual raw scenarios appear as "piles". The image clearly shows the complexity of possible futures: the rather information-technical futures are roughly located on the left side and scenarios that are characterized by strongly traditional competition are roughly located on the right side. The vertical axis goes from cars as commodity items marketed on price at the lower edge to markets based on the experience of driving, or lifestyle choices, above.

SIX SCENARIOS FOR NEW CAR DISTRIBUTION

Scenario I: Manufacturers and independent providers battle for the online market

The Internet economy has become reality. Data safety is not an issue and paying via the Net is part of daily life. Online media are not only used for pre-sales and after-sales, contracts are also concluded via the Internet. In many cases, manufacturers have gained control over the customer interface by means of attractive online offers linked with active direct distribution of their "integrated mobility" offers (e.g. at times of gluts of new cars). Most pressure is put on manufacturers by the independent portal providers, who question the old business models. A lot of former franchised dealers have been taken over by manufacturers and have been turned into service points and garages that are merely used for repairs and supply.

Scenario II: Traditional dealers manage to hold on to their customers by means of emotional brands

Consumer behaviour has not really changed: a new car stays a high-quality image bearer and is bought at the traditional franchised dealer. He offers a broad spectrum of traditional and garage services. Manufacturers have given up establishing their own direct distribution systems and are now concentrating on their core competencies in the development and production of traditional automobiles. As a countermove to this, an increasing number of dealers have linked up to build brand-oriented networks. This has finally increased the competition between brands.

Scenario III: Showdown between traditional automobile dealers

The customer has become sceptical. The colourful advertisement world of brand manufacturers no longer attracts him. His decision is based on a clearly evaluated price examination. Because automobiles have become similar, he especially watches for individual and tailor-made service offers. He can find them – as well as most new cars – at the traditional dealer who generally abstains from using online media. The portals operated by independent providers only play a minor role. Manufacturers no longer directly distribute new cars because of the minimal success rate. They concentrate on their core competencies in development and production of traditional automobiles. As a countermove, competition between garages who are tied to manufacturers by long-term contracts has increased. There is no cooperation between franchised dealers.

Scenario IV: Customer-individual automobile composition in the new car boutique

The status and prestige afforded by their automobile are of great importance to customers. They are strongly influenced by emotionally-oriented brand management, which is mainly positioned in new car boutiques directly administered by manufacturers. There is always something new to discover because the life cycles of individual automobile models have decreased further and, at the same time, automobiles have become increasingly modular. Customers can individually "put their own automobile together" through "mass customization". This development is supported by the pre-sales and after-sales services of online portals conducted by the manufacturers. Because of this development, traditional car shops have given up the lucrative services market. Linked with this, the dealer structure falls back to concentrate on the brand.

Scenario V: Competition around the experience of "mobility"

The automobile trade has changed and so has secured its position as the interface to fashion-conscious customers and customers looking for adventure. Franchised dealers who stayed in the market have associated into a strong network. This way, they – as well as some manufacturers – have been able to put their range of products into big megastores on greenfield sites. These brand worlds are customer segment-specific rather than supplier-specific. There are also new car boutiques in city centres and online offers for pre-sale and after-sales services. Here, the battle is raging between manufacturers, dealers and independent portal providers.

Scenario VI: Turning away from the brand gives a chance for the automobile discounter and service-oriented garages

The customer has become sceptical. The colourful advertisement world of brand manufacturers no longer attracts him. His decision is based on a clearly evaluated price examination. Responding to this need are mainly large automobile distributors who have sprung up and do not depend on one special brand or affiliated group. Manufacturers and independent providers put enormous emphasis on the support of their offers via online media. At the same time, specialized garages offer services at reasonable prices, and so manufacturers have not established further direct distribution networks.

USE OF THE SCENARIOS

The six scenarios were developed for use in strategic planning by car dealers, automobile manufacturers or other groups participating in the distribution of new cars. A first step was to draw out the opportunities for and threats to the various players in new car distribution. Here are two examples:

- *Car dealers:* Two separable future-robust action options emerge from the scenarios for car dealers. These are strengthening/ securing individual customer relationships and cooperation with manufacturers in e-business.

- *Automobile manufacturers:* Very different action options are suggested for automobile manufacturers. Overall, across all scenarios, drastic changes are seen, with the need for manufacturers to adopt a good early-warning system for strategic early diagnosis. Two of the future-robust options are: the establishment of own Internet portals and of e-business.

Reframing industry boundaries for structural advantage – the role of scenario planning

One of the world's largest papermakers rethinks its customer and supplier relationships after realizing that the future could be different from the past. This case study of Caledonian Paper and IPC Magazines in the paper and publishing industry was written by George Burt and Kees van der Heijden of the Centre for Scenario Planning and Future Studies, Graduate School of Business, University of Strathclyde, and is published with their permission.

BACKGROUND

This case study describes a scenario project undertaken by two organizations operating in the paper and publishing industry – Caledonian Paper and IPC Magazines. It focuses on the scenario-building process, identifying and discussing the insights participants gained from the exercise. The case study highlights the power of scenario planning to help organizations reframe the definition of their industry.

Prior to the scenario exercise, Caledonian Paper had embarked on an organization-wide project of organizational learning, with six "flagship" programmes. The scenario project was part of the customer relationships flagship programme. The objective of this programme was to develop market knowledge and a closer working relationship with their major customer, IPC Magazines. The intention was to move the relationship into the strategic arena, to help provide a better understanding of the customer's business and future needs.

IPC agreed to participate in the scenario exercise, with the aim of "joint learning to understand market dynamics and business drivers". These benefits to both parties were deemed to be: to smooth the pulp/paper price cycle and to assist planning stability for both organizations, and to broaden joint business understanding of staff across a number of functions and activities including paper production, publishing production, magazine editors and paper marketing.

SCENARIO METHODOLOGY

The scenario process was aimed at moving participants from individual understanding to developing a collective understanding across both companies, and to generate plans for action. Five stages were involved in the overall process:

- interview key players from both organizations;

- workshop to feed back information from the interview;

- scenario-development workshop;

- scenario implications and strategic options workshops;

- final presentation to participants highlighting the logic and coherence of change from the process.

This case study describes the first three stages, leading to development of the scenarios.

STAGE 1 – INTERVIEWS

The first stage involved one-to-one interviews with the key players from both organizations. The key players in this scenario project included directors and front-line operational managers with decision-making responsibility – "the scenario planners" (defined here as the participants). These interviews were analysed and merged to produce a detailed report for the participants. This stage also acted as an initial diagnostic to reveal key concerns and challenges in the minds of the participants.

The interview input led us to delineate two agendas: the internal and the external environment agenda. The internal agenda led to the development of the "Alliance" business idea. The business idea is an articulation of the history or organizational identity of the organization (van der Heijden, 1996), presented in this case as a causal loop diagram to highlight the interconnected nature of the two organizations' success formula. The external agenda highlighted the key concerns management held about the external environment.

STAGE 2 – WORKSHOP 1

The second stage was Workshop 1: feedback of the interviews and establishment of the scenario agenda. This workshop enabled participants to understand the range of views held in and across both organizations about the industry and the challenges to a closer working relationship. This was the first time that these issues had been discussed in such a format. During Workshop 1, the participants developed an agenda of themes that they felt needed to be included in the scenarios:

- consumer behaviour (including growth of electronic media, demand for lifestyle magazines);

- industry structure (considering the relationship between pulp, paper and publishing);

- macroeconomic developments (globalization and the borderless world);

- environmental influences (growth of green consumerism);

- technology (growth and role of the Internet);

- cost drivers (related to paper and publishing production);

- communication alternatives (e.g. TV, mobile phones and other small hand-held devices that could be a substitute to paper).

STAGE 3 – SCENARIO-BUILDING WORKSHOP

The scenarios were developed during a two-day workshop. A number of outside experts, known as "Remarkable people", had been invited to the workshop. "Remarkable people" are individuals who can bring new insights to help organizations better understand the themes and underlying dynamics of these problematic situations. The topics presented by the "Remarkable people" during the workshop were:

- consumer marketing and the role of new electronic media in marketing in the future; and

- the role of ICT and the drivers of value creation in society.

In addition, participants developed a system dynamics model of the pulp, paper and publishing system. Modelling this system highlighted that the system was inherently unstable and beyond the ability of either organization to control. However, more importantly, the participants recognized for the first time that the behaviour of either organization had no impact on price. Previously, both parties believed the other influenced price for their own ends. This understanding provided the basis for mutual learning during the workshop.

Triggered by this input, the participants in the workshop brainstormed on anything that might be of importance in the business environment in the future. These points (known as "nice-to-knows") were ranked on potential impact and uncertainty and from those with most impact, a framework was constructed by clustering possible outcomes into three scenarios, stories about the future of the business environment.

SCENARIO LOGICS

After ranking the various "nice to knows", the main driving forces seemed to categorize into *inside-out* and *outside-in* forces for change. Inside-out forces would be unleashed if the paper and publishing industries could work closely to collaborate on developing new channels of communication with customers. This could give a move towards greater paper price stability and better capacity management. It could also involve further alliances with companies who might have an impact on the media industry in the future. By broadening out the "Alliance", it was agreed that it would be necessary to include, for example, organizations such as telecommunication companies, banks or supermarkets. In such a case, the industry logic would be internally driven by the existing players, with the new constellations formed around the paper and publishing companies.

Outside-in forces would come to the fore if the paper and publishing industries were not in the driving seat for change, with power and control over the industry logic in the hands of *reconfigurers* such as Visa, BT, Microsoft and/or a media organization like News International. If there was continued instability of the paper price and an internal focus on cost of paper, there would be insufficient attention paid to the weak signals already existing that suggest that other media and non-media players are already redefining the industry logic.

This indicated that the industry definition or logic might be conceptualized under three separate, but interlocking circles with one locus. These circles highlight the nature of the driving forces pushing for change from the communication and media industries. The intersection of the circles is the pulp/paper/publishing industries. They will drive the change, be a partner with others in the change, or be a bystander as change occurs. All around the circles are the existing constellations of companies who are in a position today to redefine the industry logic or who will enter the picture in the future and have an impact of industry logic. In one circle, although the pulp/paper/publishing industries are the locus of change, they are also the *architects* or the drivers of change. In the second circle, the pulp/paper/publishing industries are *co-producers* of change. In the third circle, the pulp/paper/publishing industries are bystanders to change, and the *reconfigurers* are the drivers for change. This led us to use for the underlying logic of scenarios:

- industry behaviour over time – fragmented/aligned, old approach/new approach;

- penetration of electronic/new media – extent and speed.

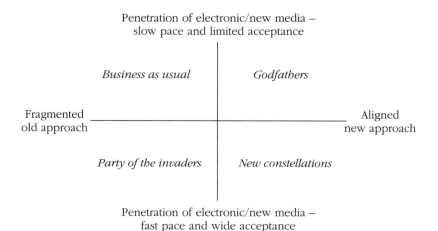

Figure IV.4.1   Paper and publishing scenario structuring matrix (reproduced by permission of George Burt and Kees van der Heijden).

During the first day of the workshop, we developed three scenarios depicting the possible futures of the pulp, paper and publishing industry cluster, in addition to "Business as Usual". The three scenarios are shown in Figure IV.4.1 and were called:

- *Godfathers*;

228

- *New constellations;*

- *Party of the invaders.*

THREE SCENARIOS

Godfathers
This scenario combines paper price stability with growth, through cooperation between the Alliance partners and the trading of pulp as a separately managed commodity. The effect of multimedia is to stimulate new markets for magazines. This stability continues in the long term as the initial successes of the Alliance bring benefits that spread within the parties to the Alliance and acts as a catalyst to greater cooperation between the parent companies. This cooperation leads to consolidation in the industry, which changes the nature of the industry logic from highly competitive and fragmented to an industry logic resembling an oligopoly.

New constellations
The *New constellations* scenario is characterized by the inability of the existing paper and publishing companies to identify, in advance, the driving forces for change that will ultimately lead to restructuring of the industry. In this scenario, power ultimately rests with the emergence of "Global Integrated Communicators" (GICs): constellations of providers such as telecommunication and advertising companies, financial service companies like Visa with their financial resources and information management expertise, consumer brand companies like Benetton with their global consumer knowledge and integrated EDI expertise, supermarket chains who understand consumer needs and who own or have access to large databases with (potential) customer information. As a consequence, the magazine industry diminishes in importance.

Party of the invaders
In this scenario, many new players emerge in the consumer communication business, and the traditional business of publishing

newspapers, books and magazines fragments into other media channels. The major feature that emerges with this fragmentation is the arrival of "Content" providers, "Service" providers and "Infrastructure" providers.

These new providers or "invaders" benefit from the inability of the paper industry to bring about stability in the price of paper. This instability results in a high cost base for publishing that makes it more difficult to launch new titles, support existing titles, or develop links with new emerging media channels. This ultimately results in the demise of the traditional publishing industry, with IPC sold to a competitor that is part of an existing partnership/alliance.

STRUCTURAL LEARNING FOR CHANGE

As Arie de Geus said: *"the ability to learn faster than the competitors may be the only sustainable competitive advantage"* (de Geus, 1999). The process of developing the three scenarios provided an opportunity for participants to enact their environment and enhance learning in both organizations. The focus of learning in this scenario project focused on three emergent themes:

• the role of ICT and reconfiguration of the supply chain;

• the role and use of ICT and electronic media for knowledge development of customers; and;

• the impact of customer empowerment through the ICT revolution.

The participants developed systemic insights previously not considered by either organization. Responding to these systemic insights ultimately resulted in changes in the participant organizations. The systemic insights highlight the power of scenario thinking.

First, participants were able to redefine the industry logic from pulp, paper and publishing to content, infrastructure and relationships. The industry value chain logic was seen to be "moving from pulp, paper and publishing to content, channels, function and distribution", then one stage further "from pulp, paper and publishing to content provider, service provider and infrastructure". This redefinition raised new questions for the participants:

- What is important for advertisers? Is it physical aspects of the product or the mode of communication?

- We are thinking vertically about the offer by putting the customer in the centre. Who can reconfigure the industry value chain?

- We have identified what we don't know. It is other industries and their impact on demand for paper (e.g. printers, electronic newspapers) that will determine our future.

- IT and the Internet are a threat to customer relationships, because of wider choice.

- The future is about communication. What is the role of paper? It is about customer dialogue and relationship.

Second, the insights challenged the dominant traditional paper production recipe. The recipe of bigger, faster paper production was ultimately shown to be obsolete in a world of customer choice and flexibility.

Finally, the participants were able to "scaffold" for knowledge developments; that is, the participants were able to connect process insights with existing knowledge to "stretch" their thinking and understanding. Suddenly, concern about closer working relationships had an underlying rationale. The participants recognized that they had a lack of interface at the point of sale that prevented the development of customer knowledge. Scarcity for these organizations was not paper or magazine titles, but access to customers to develop intelligence about future buying patterns and provision of information needs.

Participants developed insights during the scenario process from dialogue and managerial enquiry. Enquiry and questioning by the participants for structural understanding produced revelations for

231

participants: "this leads to counter-intuitive thinking – non-industry players will drive demand for paper" and "our thinking is flawed, we know little about consumers and communication" (two quotes from participants during the process).

CONCLUSION

The old saying "forewarned is forearmed" was never more apt. Scenario thinking enabled them to develop a perception about the industry beyond the "Business as Usual" view of the future. The participants were able to develop coherent business cases and argue for strategic change to ensure the survival and success of their organization: the ultimate test for any strategic management approach.

Software for collaborative working

This is a brief account of the way in which a European software business, based on a software product to support collaborative working, used a scenario approach to start a process of reframing its business. This case study was written by Tony Hodgson of IDON Ltd and is published with his permission.

THE SCENARIO PROJECT

A project team of six people consisting of individuals from marketing, sales, technology and business development started in March 1998 by brainstorming the aspects of collaborative working that a software product was expected to support. The list included:

• *community* – supporting local or virtual communities with common interests;

• *mobility* – as workers and citizens expect to have all the access they want as they move between locations, work, domestic or leisure;

• *process flow* – many business applications are in fact simple sequences of business processes and designs, based on this, support systems' evolution and maintenance more easily than traditional designs;

• *workflow* – managing a sequence of work steps and alerting managers to non-performance through software has become a standard feature of many organizations;

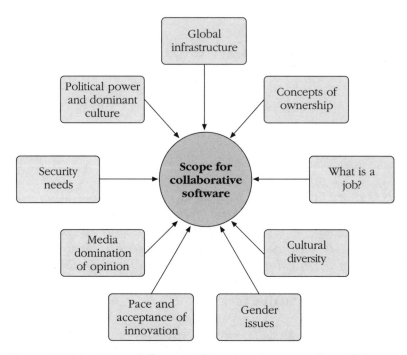

Figure IV.5.1 External factors influencing the scope for collaborative software (reproduced by permission of Tony Hodgson).

- *groupware* – supporting online communication and decisions in groups;

- *internet utilization* – a requirement that was less obvious in 1998 than later, as even internal organizational LANS use web architecture.

An initial survey among internal staff, augmented by interviews with external experts and customers, was boiled down by the project team to eight external factors that would influence the evolution of software for collaborative working (Figure IV.5.1). Around 30 people were involved.

After these preparations, a two-day residential workshop was held to think through the implications of the survey and interview material, and distil this into a set of scenarios. This consisted of the team plus another 6 people from marketing, sales, technology and business development.

Over 50 important factors prompted by Figure IV.5.1 were brainstormed by the workshop group and positioned, with much discussion, on an uncertainty/impact grid. This led to around 15 factors being selected both for their high degree of uncertainty and their more immediate impact on a collaborative working software product. These factors were more specific than those in Figure IV.5.1, which served as a check that the brainstorm was sufficiently comprehensive.

The next stage of the workshop was to apply the hexagon clustering technique (Galt, 1997) to these 15 items, which were formulated as basic uncertainties as to how the future would turn out. Two major clusters were selected as the basis for the scenario frameworks: *changing business* and *consumer power shift*.

Since each uncertainty hexagon was formulated as a "flip/flop" (i.e. it could go this way or that way), it was possible to distil out of each cluster a major bifurcation or alternate direction. One pair concerning *changing business* was between:

A CORPORATE ECOLOGY	A GLOBAL VILLAGE
In which corporate-based software with strong branding dominates how people interact	In which a high-diversity marketplace enables many enterprises to co-produce a high variety of interactive forms

The second pair on *consumer power shift* was between:

CHAMPION YOURSELF	WEST COAST HOTEL
In which the power of one can be exercised through reliable easy modular software ("home plumbing")	In which continuing system complexity enables current major competitors to continue to dominate standards and solutions

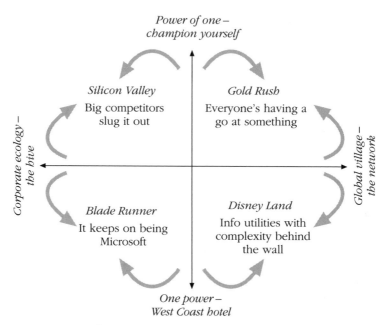

Figure IV.5.2 The environment for software-collaborative working products (reproduced by permission of Tony Hodgson).

Taking these as ends of axes, four distinct possible future worlds were suggested, as shown in Figure IV.5.2. Each quadrant represented a different scenario, which was developed with more elaborate content and backed by examples of events and trends in the current environment, and used as an indicator of future business ecology for software enterprise. At this stage of the scenario workshop, the facilitator insisted that no judgements be made as to which way the future might go. This was important to encourage imagination and lateral thinking.

Each scenario was seen to evoke a different type of dominant business model and different types of player as winners. The challenge to the team was to see how their product development strategy could be robust in all scenarios:

- The broad feeling was that *Silicon Valley* would be a battle of giants. Probably a shift from today would occur through a major disruptive technology that was held by a rapidly-growing player, probably not a current incumbent.

- *Blade Runner* was based on the anti-trust action towards Microsoft failing.

- *Disney Land* might just as well have been AOL land in that it is the control of the networks that is the crux here.

- *Gold Rush* is more in the vein of the development of the Linux operating system and the phenomena of open source software freely available. However, it also assumed that software became at least as easy to do as home plumbing with standard components and easy joints.

The output from the workshop was visually captured and then edited into working documents and presentations that were used to evaluate a strategic marketing exercise based on the Chasm Model of Geoffrey Moore (1992).

REFLECTIONS

What are the changes over the last four years? The jury is still out despite some partially defining events, and the field of collaborative work is still very much in its early days, both technologically and socially.

Changes

- The internet and .com revolution certainly exploded into a global village trend.

- The corporate world has widely adopted Internet and web technology, for intranets and knowledge sharing.

- Despite the current financial problems of telecoms, the power of networks is growing rather than diminishing.

- All this is further sent spinning by the new security needs for global systems and the potential for criminalization and terrorization.

What has not changed

- The tension between "power of one" and "one power" is still alive and well.

- The consolidation and commoditization of the computer industry may yet open the way for the information appliance.

Foresight into insight

Texaco used scenarios over a period of four years to make better strategic decisions and develop new business opportunities, working with Peter Schwartz of Global Business Network. This is an excerpt from a case study describing how Texaco's Strategic Management Group (SMG) used the scenario process, helping to create the context for investment and policy decisions by the company, over an approximately four-year period from 1997. This excerpt focuses on the aspects of the project that provide lessons for managers on engagement with executives and business units, fostering strategic conversation and aligning the organization to respond to emerging challenges. It is reproduced by permission of Texaco.

BACKGROUND

Texaco is a global energy company with operations in more than 150 countries. It earned $2.5 billion on revenues of $51.1 billion in 2000. In 1997, the new CEO, Peter Bijur, asked SMG to identify the challenges and opportunities over the next 10–15 years. Drew Overpeck solicited for assistance from Global Business Network (GBN), and a "collaborative" scope of work was developed. A classic scenarios exercise was launched with interviews commencing in mid-1997 and the first workshop was held in October 1997. This identified the focal question:

*What are the long-term **structural** options for Texaco's participation and **leadership** in the **energy** industry?*

239

Figure IV.6.1   Initial scenario construct (reproduced by permission of Texaco).

After consideration of a large number of drivers and forces for change, a consensus emerged around two drivers: the nature of *business models* (whether customer driven or asset driven); and the nature of *markets* (whether global and open or closed and restrictive). The quadrants resulting from Figure IV.6.1 suggested four distinct worlds. The growth of environmental values was viewed as inevitable and applicable across the board.

Deductive vs. inductive approach

Workshop participants were dissatisfied, however, with the seemingly rigid nature of the matrix and the distinct scenarios it suggested. The world is more fluid, they pointed out, with drivers that interact with one another and have an influence in more than one quadrant. Furthermore, the scenarios had lost much of the richness of story threads developed earlier, particularly around values systems (e.g. environmentalism, isolationism).

The GBN facilitators proposed that the *deductive* matrix be abandoned in favour of a more *inductive* approach, using clusters of the driving forces identified earlier as building blocks to develop stories about how the future might unfold.

Creating consensus

Three distinct views emerged that painted a more fluid and dynamic picture of the future business environment for Texaco.

There was consensus around *one* set of drivers, which was seen as reshaping relations between energy companies and host countries in the future. "Access to resources" (read oil and gas reserves) would likely be impacted by the policies of host governments and state oil company ambitions for an expanded role. Also critical would be US Government foreign policy, given its propensity for unilateral action that often ends up putting US companies at a disadvantage.

There was consensus around a *second* set of drivers, which involved changing relationships between customers, vendors and product or service providers. New competitors, new brands and new distribution channels were threatening the market share of incumbent players. These "invaders" could relegate energy companies to the low-margin commodity or asset end of the business, preventing them from enjoying their traditional rents from various elements of the value chain.

Finally, there was consensus around a *third* set of converging drivers. Environmental pressures, societal values and technological change were viewed as interacting to bring about change in consumer demand. Concerns about greenhouse gas emissions and climate change, social expectations of corporate responsibility and the development of new or alternative propulsion systems and energy carriers were seen as likely to reshape the energy mix of the future.

A *fourth* set of drivers was rejected by near-unanimous vote. It revolved around domestic and global unrest, and anti-American sentiment stemming from a clash between the "haves" and the "have-nots". It seemed to deviate from an energy focus and was viewed by many attendees as not being relevant or credible with a corporate audience who had never experienced a scenario-planning process. In hindsight, the process should have been trusted as it pointed to the emerging issue of anti-globalization.

Developing the story outlines

The workshop broke up into three groups to create a story around each of the scenarios, considering what geopolitical or policy changes might occur, when new energy technologies might make major inroads, and how social values and business models might change. The approach was predominantly *qualitative* and anecdotal, as this was seen as being better able to communicate the dynamic complexity of drivers and future uncertainties.

The first workshop ended with a discussion of the plausibility and robustness of the scenarios, and the action steps, work plan and research agenda needed to be undertaken to go forward.

ENRICHING THE VIEWS AND DEVELOPING THE CHALLENGES

The second workshop
The second scenario workshop was held at the same off-site resort location in early December 1997, with most of the original participants in attendance. The aims of the workshop were to validate and test the scenarios, to use the scenario framework to develop implications for the industry and to focus on the implications these different worlds might have for Texaco.

The scenarios were initially depicted as a series of concentric triangles (Figure IV.6.2) with each side representing the relevant business environment and industry drivers.

Industry implications
Following the discussion of the scenarios, participants spent the next day and a half of the workshop brainstorming the implications.

The *New nationalism* scenario, for example, suggested that some state oil companies could evolve into international players in competition or alliance with the international majors. Host governments, seeking to balance self-determination desires with the need for investment and technology, would likely restructure relationships with multinationals. Today's players would likely have to create new value propositions as "connectors" in order to compete and meet the higher expectations of host governments. Companies may be transformed from reserve equity holders into service providers and be valued accordingly. Relationships would be crucial.

The *Energy solutions* scenario suggested that, as margins

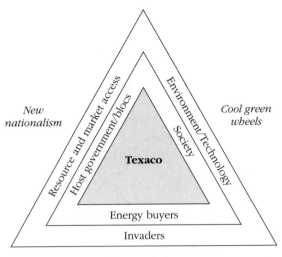

Energy solutions

Figure IV.6.2 Texaco corporate scenarios (initial diagram) (reproduced by permission of Texaco).

migrated toward the customer end of the value chain, intimate customer knowledge would likely become key. There could be a shift from products to offerings, as a few consumer brands became dominant and sought to bundle energy and other utility services for customers. Fuel providers could end up being relegated to the commodity (low margin) end of the business. Customer drivers would obviously differ in mature vs. developing markets.

The *Cool green wheels* scenario suggested that, as social values were reflected in public policy and the demand for cleaner fuels grew, energy companies should adjust their portfolios toward lower-carbon resources. Accordingly, companies should look to natural gas plays in the USA and overseas, as well as seek opportunities in alternate energy technologies. Companies would also benefit from a greener brand and active engagement with non-governmental organizations.

Implications for Texaco
Suggested long-term strategies included a repositioning of the Texaco brand, a rethinking of leadership and relationship skills,

and a need to reperceive the value chain and consider a role as a service provider or "connector". Participants also addressed the importance of monitoring and investing in new energy technology developments, and rethinking certain policy stances.

The second workshop ended with a listing of next steps, which included a need to quantify the scenarios, strengthen the business case and conduct additional research on, for instance, the potential economic impacts of each scenario in terms of changes in GDP growth rates, energy supply and demand, and oil prices.

Reference case

As a reference, the team created a "business as usual" scenario that articulated Texaco's official view of the future. Entitled *Continuing global integration,* the scenario described a future world of sustained economic growth with a steady expansion in the demand for oil and other fuels.

The scenario held that, despite technological change and increasing environmental regulation, oil would continue to dominate the transportation market. OPEC would remain a loose cartel, and oil prices, though volatile, would continue to be significantly above free-market levels.

The reference case essentially described a future world without radical shifts in technology, business models or geopolitics.

FINALIZING THE CHALLENGES

The third workshop

A third workshop involving fewer participants was held in mid-January 1998 to compare the scenarios in final form, further develop the thoughts on industry and Texaco implications, and recommend individual strategies and actions. The team was also intent on identifying the *common* implications that would suggest robust across-the-board strategies for Texaco.

Workshop participants suggested that Texaco consider the set of options: *Watch and Wait, Watch and Prepare or Lead the Charge* for each scenario. Particularly, the company should consider what it would mean for Texaco to be a leader or prime mover.

Participants also recognized that, while it was important to examine how Texaco should behave within each scenario, the rest of the world was not going to come to a standstill. Finally, workshop participants brainstormed some "signposts" or early warning signals for each scenario. They pointed out that these would be important for Texaco's strategic planners to monitor, in order to track whether one scenario or another (or a combination) was unfolding.

Making it relevant
In the weeks following the third workshop, the team wrestled with how best to communicate the scenarios and their implications to an executive audience that was sure to be more interested in the insights and recommendations rather than the scenarios themselves. Their challenge was how to capture the executives' attention and make it relevant to business needs.

The team decided to downplay the scenarios and focus instead on the corporate challenges facing Texaco, as well as its options and strategic alternatives. This shift in focus was responsible for much of the subsequent success of the project roll-out.

CHALLENGES FOR THE FUTURE

Shifts in control
The final presentation was entitled *Shifts in Control: Confronting Our Strategic Challenges*. Its central theme reflected another key insight: that Texaco was in danger of losing control of its destiny as value and margins shifted from owning assets to owning relationships, from relying on contractual protections to leveraging deep-seated proprietary knowledge, and from an industrial age business model to one based in the information age.

At its outset, the presentation spelled out three key challenges to Texaco's future success:

- that access to and ownership of exploration and producing opportunities may be constrained by the politics of the host countries and actions of the US government;

- that new intruders may get between Texaco and its customers, taking away its marketing margins, and leaving the traditional industry with the commodity part of the business; and

- that environmental pressures and technological change may converge with changing social values and lead to major shifts in the mix of fuels used to produce energy in all forms.

The clear message was that the relatively assured margins that Texaco had traditionally enjoyed were likely to erode over time as society, technology, geopolitics and business models changed. Notwithstanding a continuing emphasis on its core business, the company was going to have to adapt its business models and strategies to respond and stay in the game.

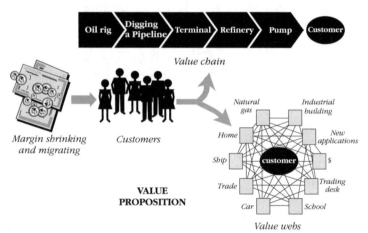

Figure IV.6.3 The location of "value" is shifting (reproduced by permission of Texaco).

An example of this ongoing evolution is reflected in Figure IV.6.3. Customers expect and are being offered new value propositions, as value chains disintegrate and are replaced by value "webs". As a result, margins are shrinking and migrating towards the customer.

Margins could be further eroded by the threat from new "invaders" and disruptive technology that could eventually eclipse existing technologies. The challenge for Texaco is to be alert to such shifts and invest in the right opportunities.

What's in a name

Seeking clarity, the team revisited the name of each scenario to ensure that it truly reflected its key challenge. Accordingly, the *New nationalism* scenario was renamed *By invitation only* to reflect the likelihood that access to reserves would be at the discretion of host governments.

The scenario entitled *Energy solutions* was renamed *The new go-betweens* to reflect a future where new market entrants or "invaders" might supplant existing players and seek to "own the customer", so as to capture margins that were migrating to the retail end of the value chain.

The third scenario on environmental values and technology, originally called *Cool green wheels*, was renamed *Multiple-choice energy* to reflect the likelihood that a mosaic of technologies and fuels would emerge, requiring energy companies to meet a range of customer needs.

Summary graphic

The three scenarios and their respective challenges were depicted in a summary graphic (Figure IV.6.4), which was later used with various audiences. Each of the triangle's three sides reflects the central "shift in control" taking place, together with its drivers and key challenge.

Communicating the message

Early on, the team realized that conveying its findings to a Texaco audience would require a multi-pronged communications plan that was focused yet flexible, and relevant to managers attuned to shorter-term views. Accordingly, the team set about creating communications materials and devising a strategy to resonate with target audiences. The team spent time researching and quantifying the potential magnitude of the shifts taking place to ensure that the key messages were taken seriously. It also documented the "size of the prize" in terms of the value of potential opportunities for Texaco. The presentation also incorporated specific recommendations on how Texaco could respond to these challenges. These included strategies to improve relationships with customers, host

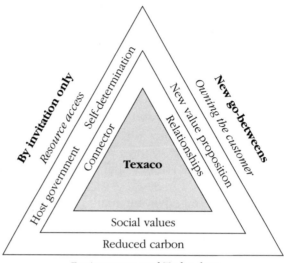

Figure IV.6.4 Texaco corporate scenarios (final summary diagram) (reproduced by permission of Texaco).

governments and non-governmental organizations, as well as to explore new business models, and invest in emerging technologies.

The team procured several props for use during the presentation to drive home the main points even further. These included a Mobil *Speedpass*, a computer silicon-wafer motherboard, and several news articles, as evidence of the changes taking place. The scenarios and background material were compiled into a comprehensive master document. This was distilled into a 12-page executive summary document for distribution across the company.

Additionally, the team created a set of workshop templates for business units to enable them to consider the unique implications of the scenarios for the future of their own business.

Pursuing additional avenues of communication, the team partnered with the Human Resource Department's *Organizational Effectiveness* (OE) group, who work to improve standards of leadership at Texaco. The scenarios were integrated into OE's advanced leadership training materials.

As a result of presentations to the CEO in March 1998 and other members of the senior leadership at Texaco, the team found that these audiences were more interested in the qualitative than the quantitative aspects, a surprise in the numbers-oriented Texaco culture.

The team also took the presentation on the road, speaking to key Texaco audiences including business unit planning groups, scientific and technical fellows, executive business analysts, and public and government affairs professionals.

The scenarios and their attendant challenges were reflected in the keynote address that Peter Bijur gave to the 17th Congress of the World Energy Council on 14 September 1998 (Bijur, 1998). The speech was lauded for its vision, and has since been cited repeatedly for its insights into the changes still taking place in the industry.

REVALIDATING THE FUTURE

Shifts in control II
In late 1999, concerned that the scenarios might be nearing the limit of their usefulness, SMG set out to revisit them and, if needed, create a new set of scenarios. In testing the validity of the original scenarios, though, the team concluded that they were still robust and relevant.

The team found evidence that the scenarios were, in fact, unfolding as described earlier, and in many instances faster than foreseen. Given their impact on Texaco's businesses, it was even more important that they be factored into the company's plans.

The team did conclude, however, that *globalization* had emerged as one challenge that had not been clearly identified earlier. Building on globalization scenarios generated by GBN, the team conducted a workshop to examine the forces driving globalization, its tensions, alternative outcomes and long-term implications for Texaco.

IMPACT ON THE FUTURE

Pursuing additional knowledge

The scenarios and challenges served as a launch pad for numerous initiatives; for example:

- On the *geopolitical* front, there were investigations into the structure of the Russian oil industry and its companies, into Venezuela and Brazil, and the other major oil companies; scenarios for the Pacific Rim, China and the Middle East, and key countries in the Middle East were also studied.

- From a *technology* standpoint, SMG studied the decarbonization of fuels and the emerging hydrogen economy. This included analyses of alternative technology vehicles, fuel cells and distributed power generation, as well as the mosaic of potential fuels and related infrastructure, and existing global energy resources, including reserves, supply, demand and potential substitutes (e.g. renewable energy options such as wind and solar power).

- With respect to the *environment*, SMG used a scenarios approach to analyse global warming and climate change, the alternative ways in which this issue could unfold and Texaco's options.

- SMG also led a study of sustainable development and corporate social responsibility issues.

Creating the strategic context

The scenarios and related research created the "strategic context" for a number of subsequent investment and policy decisions at Texaco. A few are highlighted below:

- The company created Texaco Energy Systems Inc. (TESI) in 1999 to explore opportunities in fuel cells, hydrocarbons-to-liquids and alternative fuels.

- In mid-2000, Texaco purchased a 20 per-cent stake in Energy

Conversion Devices (ECD), with a view to commercializing "green" energy technologies.

- The scenarios enabled Texaco to revisit its policies on climate change. The study of how this issue could unfold prompted Texaco to withdraw from the Global Climate Coalition and launch a greenhouse gas emissions management programme.

- The study of sustainable development enabled Texaco's policy makers to better appreciate the changing societal expectations of multinational corporations and key elements of above-ground risk. As a result, Texaco was able to reposition itself and is now included in the Dow Jones Sustainability Group Index.

Conclusions and reflections

The scenarios generated corporate-wide awareness of the challenges and opportunities Texaco faces in a rapidly-changing business environment. They enabled management to make far-reaching portfolio, investment and policy decisions. Several of these were beyond the scope of any one business unit.

The corporate scenario process was a valuable learning experience. Notwithstanding the CEO's support, the team realized that executive endorsement was no guarantee of buy-in. As a result, team members had personally to champion initiatives in which they believed.

In pursuing a pioneering role that was somewhat separate from Texaco's traditional planning process, SMG found that it had traded relevance for independence. It was difficult to make the scenarios and their implications relevant to managers driven by nearer-term business metrics.

Notwithstanding executive interest in the qualitative, SMG also found that it was dealing with a corporate mindset that valued numerical estimates over concepts and ideas. The team had to be creative to navigate its way through a corporate culture that was more comfortable with "business as usual" thinking than "outside the box".

Some business unit managers were sceptical of the usefulness of the scenario process and were unwilling to commit resources. For the projects that did move forward, SMG found it had constantly to emphasize the *external* perspective to counter the tendency to focus on the internal. The benefits were later obvious.

SMG realized that the scenarios were not an end in themselves, but a means to an end in terms of the implications and challenges they evoked. As a consequence, SMG was careful in its use of the term "scenario", preferring instead to refer to "challenges" and "strategic alternatives".

The scenarios and their implications appeared to resonate with most audiences. The challenge for SMG, however, was getting key decision makers to initiate responsive action. Tighter focus on relevance and a robust communication strategy may have increased effectiveness.

Pursuing additional avenues of communication to penetrate the domain of the key decision makers, the team partnered with the Human Resource department's *Organizational Effectiveness* (OE) group that works to improve standards of leadership at Texaco. The scenarios were integrated into OE's advanced leadership training materials.

Furthermore, time and again SMG found it challenging to get audiences to focus on the evolving needs of the end-*consumer.* SMG suspected that this was probably the result of a dominant engineering or asset-oriented mindset at Texaco and the predominant B2B business model.

On a positive note, SMG worked hard to engage and cultivate a select group of like-minded individuals from across Texaco at the corporate and business unit level. This ensured wide input and diverse perspective, and provided a base of internal support for key agendas.

Finally, though the original scenarios covered a 10–15-year period, change has occurred more rapidly than anticipated. The pace of geopolitical shifts, environmental policy changes, new energy technologies and revamped customer–vendor relationships has generally accelerated.

This speaks to the need to revisit and keep scenarios updated. It also highlights the difficulty of setting aside one's implicit biases to look beyond the immediate horizon, while still retaining relevance to a highly competitive business.

Healthcare 2010 scenarios: guiding a vision for predictive medicine

GlaxoSmithKline used scenarios to explore futures for health services in order to decide their role in those futures and to encourage their preferred future to develop. Clem Bezold of the Institute for Alternative Futures (IAF) facilitated the project. This case study has been written by Paul Meade, Vice-President of Best Practices LLC and Clement Bezold, PhD of the Institute for Alternative Futures.

BACKGROUND

The chairman of Glaxo Wellcome (now GlaxoSmithKline), Dr Richard Sykes, was contemplating the entry of the company into the area of diagnostics. Taking a long-term view of the company's future, he knew genetics would play a critical role in the future of health care. Since genetics would one day allow the "prediction" of probable disease profiles among people, it was important that Glaxo Wellcome take a serious look at the field of diagnostics and prognostics, from simple blood tests to sophisticated imaging technology. Since this was unfamiliar territory, Dr Sykes asked his R&D department to evaluate whether Glaxo Wellcome should become directly involved in diagnostics.

A diagnostics evaluation team was created, with members from the research, commercial and finance divisions within Glaxo Wellcome. This team met regularly over a several-month period and recommended that Glaxo Wellcome should move into the area of diagnostics and create a group dedicated to developing this capability, as opposed to going out and acquiring an existing diagnostic company.

In January 1999, when the Predictive Medicine Group was formed within the R&D organization of Glaxo Wellcome, the first task was to develop a vision, a mission and long-range goals.

A worldwide Director, Ian Gilham, and a worldwide Commercial Director, Paul Meade, headed the Predictive Medicine Group. They commissioned Clem Bezold of Alternative Futures Associates (AFA), the for-profit subsidiary of IAF, to serve as the "vision coach" and to assist in developing scenarios for the future of health care. These scenarios led to the development of a vision, a mission and some long-range goals for the Predictive Medicine Group, which are currently being implemented within the newly-merged company, GlaxoSmithKline.

Building the team

To accomplish the first task of the Predictive Medicine Group, a new team was created that would explore the integration of therapeutics and diagnostics. Named the Therapeutics and Diagnostics Integration Project Team (TDIP), it comprised members from research, genetics, commercial, finance, strategy planning and business development plus Clem Bezold. The mandate of TDIP was to:

1. look at the future of health care and the pharmaceutical industry;

2. determine how therapeutics, genetics and diagnostics will integrate in the future; and

3. develop a vision, a mission and long-range goals for the Predictive Medicine Group.

Trying to predict the future of health care over the next 10 years was no mean task, particularly as the map of the human genome was making serious progress. Scenarios provided the best tool to accomplish the objectives. Since only two team members had had previous experience in developing scenarios, educating the team on the development and use of scenarios was the first assignment. This education step is crucial for any team undertaking the creation of scenarios, since many people misunderstand the intended use or underestimate the complexity of developing sound scenarios. Taking the time to explain the process of scenario building to the entire team may have seemed counterproductive at first, but it went a long way in averting potential frustrations among some team members. Dealing with a complex set of uncertainties and possibilities during the construction of long-range scenarios can otherwise push the uninitiated into their "uncomfort zone", which can ultimately lead to a disruption of the team's progress.

Once the training was complete, the team was ready to tackle mapping out potential global futures for health care.

Creating the scenarios

The context for the scenarios was the accepted premise that sometime in the near future we will be able to predict with some accuracy:

1. who is likely to develop a particular disease;

2. how therapeutic regimens will work differently in different individuals; and

3. the likely outcome of such therapeutic interventions.

Health care and the pharmaceutical industry are likely to see dramatic changes over the next decade. Key drivers of change include the health of the population, the economic state of countries, health-care policy, the pace and direction of disease knowledge, and the enormous impact of genetics. There are uncertainties surrounding each of these, and scenarios bound the uncertainty of the future by defining likely pathways, both for health care and the pharmaceutical industry.

The team spent the first several weeks gathering information from a broad range of sources on a variety of topics such as demographics, society, economics, politics, epidemiology, medical technologies, communication technologies, environmental factors, bioethics and health-care policy, and global health-care delivery. These drivers of change were aggregated and clustered into "macro" categories. The drivers of change were then prioritized by scoring each of them with a separate rating for probability of occurring and likely impact on business.

The next step was then to take those drivers with the highest scores in each category and begin to develop projections over a 10-year period. These described both negative and positive impacts on the business. For instance, if the driver were data confidentiality, a negative projection would be that no genetic information on patients with a particular disease would ever be made available to researchers in a pharmaceutical company for purposes of finding new cures. On the other hand, a positive projection would be that a patient's genetic profile would be readily available for research purposes and for designing customized treatment programmes, with the corresponding protections for privacy and against discrimination in place.

Once projections for the key forces were completed with a reasonable amount of background information to support them, they were then reprioritized in order of importance (i.e. likelihood and impact) and clustered in a variety of sequences such as some negative aspects of some trends with positive aspects of others.

These projections were the progenitors of the scenarios. For some scenario-generation efforts, it makes sense to let a small number of variables lead to a matrix that defines the scenarios. However, since health care over the next 10 years is likely to be seriously impacted by several drivers of change, a more complex methodology was used to develop our scenarios, a multivariate sequencing approach.

Following the guidance of the vision coach on never having an odd number of scenarios and never having too many, the team "distilled" the trend projections into four primary scenarios that followed IAF/AFA's "archetypical" pattern (i.e. best guess, hard times and two paradigm shift scenarios, at least one of which is "visionary").

THE SCENARIOS

The scenarios primarily focused on health care and, to a lesser extent, the development and deployment of genomics knowledge and tools. The four health-care scenarios were:

- *Health-care gains continue – a familiar environment with steady advances and growing competition for conventional health care and providers:*
  - ○ knowledge in genetics progresses at current pace;
  - ○ Rx/Dx/Gx integration slow to come (Rx = therapeutics, Dx = diagnostics and Gx = genetics);
  - ○ some significant breakthroughs, but not many;
  - ○ Health-care delivery predominantly via physicians;
  - ○ consumers gain knowledge through Internet;
  - ○ demand for medicines increases;
  - ○ many approvals of new drugs but margins erode due to cost pressures;
  - ○ increased use of alternative medicines.

- *Recessions slow health gains – slowdown in the economy with a concomitant decline in pharmaceutical advances:*
  - ○ two significant recessions stall health-care innovations and slow R&D in pharmaceuticals;
  - ○ global economic pressures erode margins on medicines with fewer medicines approved;
  - ○ genetics has a major setback due to failure to deliver, experiment disaster and data privacy issues;
  - ○ alternative medicines flourish;
  - ○ accelerated consolidation in the pharmaceutical industry.

- *Integrated biosciences pay off – many advances, more complex markets and integration of Rx, Dx, and Gx:*
  - ○ Rx/Dx/Gx becomes fully integrated;
  - ○ advances in medical technology have the effect of changing health-care delivery to disease prediction and prevention;
  - ○ consumers partner with physicians to manage health and wellness and make use of CHPs (Certified Health Planners);
  - ○ treatment focus is subsymptomatic;
  - ○ many products become available quickly, but margins are lower;
  - ○ pharmaceutical companies emphasize services, over products.

- *Globalhealth.com – significant health services and public health success in raising health outcomes globally through web-based technologies:*
  - ○ the Internet has a major impact on health care – e-health and global health come together as globalhealth.com;
  - ○ consumers are key drivers and decision makers in health care;
  - ○ geographic borders dissolve and the world becomes a virtual community subdivided by genotypes;
  - ○ "cybervisits" to health-care providers are common;
  - ○ e-Rx commoditizes pharmaceuticals;
  - ○ pharmaceutical companies partner with non-traditional players;
  - ○ cooperative social values globally drive national health-care policies (concern for diseases everywhere);
  - ○ pharmaceutical companies sell outcomes services.

USING THE SCENARIOS

Once the scenarios were developed and well understood by each team member, the next step in the process was to construct a comparative matrix. This was accomplished by simply listing each of the four scenarios across the top of the page and then placing each of the key drivers of change down the left-hand side. Reading vertically down the scenario column gives a sense of the total impact of the scenario, while reading horizontally across the drivers gives a sense of the range of potential variation.

When there is only a small variation in the projection for the driver in three or four scenarios, it suggests that the trend is relatively certain within the "core of plausibility" defined by these four scenarios. If such is the case, then that driver of change has to be considered a critical element of any long-range strategy as likely to impact the business.

The next use of the comparative matrix is to look for significant "outliers". In other words, a given driver might have a large impact on a particular scenario, but not on any of the others. This is a driver that requires special attention, either as a "trigger" for the scenario to unfold, or as an element to watch should the scenario begin to manifest over time.

The matrix serves a useful role in extracting optimal value from the scenarios. Drivers that appear significantly impactful *across* scenarios require particular attention in developing implications and strategies, whereas drivers that have a major impact in only one scenario could be used to develop special contingency plans for a strategy.

After careful analysis of the health-care environment using the scenarios and the comparative matrix, the TDIP team was ready to begin identifying key capabilities and potential long-range strategies for the Predictive Medicine Group.

The team guarded against picking its "favourite scenario" from among the four. Given the uncertainties of health care over the next 10 years explored in the four plausible scenarios, the team then developed its preferred future: the ideal future to create for the Predictive Medicine group, including how much of an impact the group should have in creating this positive future in the industry.

The team also discussed how quickly the Predictive Medicine Group could achieve realistic goals and what the top priorities would be to focus on in the short term.

After several more weeks, the team began to create a draft of their long-term goals, strategies, priorities and capabilities. These gave birth to a mission statement and, ultimately, a vision. Make no mistake about the painstaking effort that should go into a vision statement: it should take into consideration the long-term possibilities of an uncertain business environment, but also contain an element of "future shaping". Yet, it is important to remember that *vision without action is hallucination* and *action without vision is a nightmare.*

After exhaustive reviews of the trends, forecasts and scenarios, and endless hours of debating the precise wording of these statements, the TDIP team created the Predictive Medicine Group's vision and mission.

THE VISION

Improving lifelong health through predictive knowledge.

THE MISSION

Predictive Medicine will contribute to improving health outcomes through predictive knowledge and add value to Glaxo Wellcome's innovative medicines and services by integrating novel diagnostics and prognostics with appropriate therapeutic interventions.

In addition to the vision and mission statements, the team also developed long-range goals, the overall strategy and the core competencies for the Predictive Medicine Group. The last responsibility of the TDIP team was to present the findings and recommendations to the Predictive Medicine Board and later to the Executive Committee at Glaxo Wellcome.

Presenting the scenarios

Presenting scenarios of plausible futures 10 years ahead to an audience that spends most of their working hours dealing with operational duties, decision making on immediate tactics and other administrative activities of a large organization is hard. In fact, it is difficult to take any individual from their world of "today" and transport them to a world 10 years on, especially one as complex as health care. The team had to find a clever and novel way to bring the Predictive Medicine Board into the future, literally to catapult them 10 years into the future of health-care delivery, and not just the future of the pharmaceutical industry.

The team chose a simulated television interview with a fictitious author of a book called *The Fifth Colony*. This author is being interviewed by a TV talk-show host about his best-seller written about four colonists who left planet Earth 10 years before, in the year 2000, to go and establish a health-care delivery system on each of their respective colonies on distant planets. Each colonist established a health-care system based on the common knowledge they departed with in the year 2000, yet each system developed quite differently from each other.

The scenarios were presented to the Predictive Medicine Board through a play-acting simulation involving various TDIP team members. One member of the team was the TV talk-show host, another the famous author of the book and four other team members acted as colonists invited on the show to be interviewed by the host.

The TV host questioned the author first about his book *The Fifth Colony* and his reason for writing such an interesting book. The author stated how he was intrigued by the fact that four people, armed with the exact same knowledge of health care in 2000, left Earth to form a health-care system that differed so much from each other only 10 years later. After a few general questions to the author about the four different health-care systems (i.e. the scenarios), the TV host then invited representatives from each of the four colonies to "come on stage" to answer a few questions. The colonists describe various drivers of change each encountered on their colony and how these drivers impacted the evolution of their health-care system. Hence, the four scenarios were unfolded before the Board in a "believable" fashion, and the Board members were invited to ask questions of the four colonists.

In the end, the TV host turned to the author and asked how he had arrived at the title, *The Fifth Colony*, since there were only four colonies. To which he replied, "The Fifth Colony refers to the ideal future we would have created had we known what these colonists learned over the past 10 years."

The TDIP team, having "set the stage" for the four scenarios of health care in 2010, then outlined to the Board the vision, the mission, the overall strategy and the long-range goals for the Predictive Medicine Group.

Implementation plan

The Predictive Medicine Board fully endorsed the strategic direction and long-range goals for the Predictive Medicine Group. The Group then went on to present these recommendations to the Executive Committee at Glaxo Wellcome. Likewise, the Committee accepted and gave full support to the Predictive Medicine Group in implementing the goals and strategies.

Members of the Predictive Medicine Group then developed the core capabilities, and the long-range goals were used to develop shorter-term objectives and key priorities. Immediately following the conclusions of the TDIP team, the Predictive Medicine Group implemented a company-wide communication plan. The purpose of this communication plan was to create an awareness of the Group and to "get everyone on board" with the vision, mission and strategy of the Predictive Medicine Group, so they, in turn, could understand and support the efforts of the Group.

The scenarios were rewritten in a condensed version, printed as a brochure and distributed throughout the company. Other groups within GlaxoSmithKline have used these health-care scenarios to assist them in their efforts to create divisional goals and strategies. Each of the TDIP team members made themselves available to anyone in the company either to explain in greater detail the individual scenarios, or to assist in the process of developing their own modified scenarios or goals. In November 2000, the scenarios were also publicly released at an industry genomics conference, as well as to the UK government to assist with their planning for a future health-care delivery system.

The team developed "signposts" for use in monitoring the movement toward one or the other of the scenarios, which Business Development is using to seek new business opportunities to support the creation of the ideal future for the Predictive Medicine Group.

Discussions held afterwards with TDIP team members indicated that the entire process was a learning and rewarding experience, and really helped them "anticipate" future possibilities. Several team members and members of the Predictive Medicine Group were invited to present these scenarios to other groups within the company. In addition, these scenarios were also presented to various external health-care groups through conferences and seminars.

LEARNING POINTS

- Developing a vision for part of an organization needs input from right across the organization, to ensure coherence with overall strategy.

- Taking the time to familiarize team members with scenario thinking repays the investment.

- Scenarios travel best with those familiar with their source, however good the documentation, especially if follow-up action is required.

- Synthetic futures, derived after the creation of scenarios, are useful in setting action plans.

A trading group

A short workshop for the trading group, based on existing scenarios for the City of London, helped the Group to analyse their portfolio by exposing the differing default scenarios of business unit management teams.

BACKGROUND

The group's origins went back to the 1700s, trading sugar from the Caribbean into the USA and worldwide. Headquartered in the UK, the business extended over the years from sugar into other products, from trading to refining and sourcing, and into stockbroking, investment management and insurance. The business operated as a partnership for many years until it was floated on the London Stock Exchange.

In 1999, Gill Ringland was asked whether scenarios could help the group anticipate changes in markets: recent swings in sugar prices had impacted them badly. Various approaches were discussed, from a conventional scenario-building workshop for senior managers, to a briefing on scenarios and role playing by the managers based on "what are our strengths in each of the following scenarios". The group decided to take the second approach using existing scenarios and to take advantage of an off-site planning meeting of the finance teams of each of the businesses, to introduce scenario thinking and to help analyse the group's portfolio of businesses. Though this meant that they only had four hours out of a two-day meeting, it had the great advantage of building the workshop into the finance team's mainstream activities.

The businesses ranged from a division focused on the sourcing, delivery and distribution of agricultural products to end-users around the world, including food and beverage manufacturers, farmers and other industrial users, to divisions engaged in trading futures in a number of markets and others providing investment and insurance services.

CHOOSING A SET OF SCENARIOS

The scenarios chosen were those first introduced by Richard O'Brien of Global Business Network in *London in 2020* (Ringland, 1998) for the future of financial services in the City of London.

These scenarios were based on the assumptions: that, in 2020, English would dominate even more than in 1999, that many organizations would work across three time zones – the USA, Europe and Asia – and that the privatization of the public sector and welfare (e.g. pensions) across Europe would lead to increased demand for financial services. But how would financial services develop?

Two important factors would be the extent of globalization and the adoption of technology:

- How global would financial services be?

- What would the role of technology be?

The four scenarios encapsulating possible answers to these questions are shown in Figure IV.8.1:

- *Globetech* is a world in which technology is widely used within a well-regulated environment. Stock trading is global, and the City of London dominates the European time zone for trading.

- The *Fragtech* world is dominated by the threats of IT, the problems of data protection and security. Markets are fragmented, and, though the City of London is at the front end, much of the trading is done on other markets.

- *Fourth world* foresaw the effect if, for instance, the Y2K meltdown had occurred as predicted by some pundits: technology would be seen to have failed, and the City of London would be mostly trading UK shares in a fragmented Europe.

- In the world of *Slowglobe*, airlines and telecom companies do well as travel and faxes are needed to replace technology that doesn't do the job: though markets are global, local operations are needed in many locations to ensure business continuity.

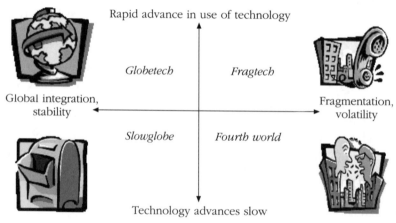

Figure IV.8.1 Technology and globalization.

THE WORKSHOP

The workshop was organized to take a full afternoon. It started with a short briefing on scenarios and forecasts, the use of scenarios by similar financial services companies, and technology and globalization scenarios. The team then split into business units to examine:

How would our business do if each of these scenarios were to come to pass? The units looked at such aspects as competition, size and growth of market, and barriers to entry in each of the scenarios. The answers were very different for each business.

The division trading primary and secondary products felt comfortable with *Slowglobe*, based on their experience in the business (e.g. the need to inspect the quality of goods on the ground). Other businesses had built their business plan on assumptions corresponding to *Globetech*, *Fragtech* and *Fourth World*.

The discussion at report-back from each unit was very revealing to the business and teams: they had not realized the very different dynamics of the businesses and the range of default scenarios and tacit assumptions within the group. In particular, the division concerned with ownership of land, refineries and the logistical needs of handling the products had a very different dynamic from the other businesses, which relied on trading, albeit with different strengths and geographic reach.

LATER EVENTS

In 2000, the group separated into two parts along the lines seen in the discussion of the scenarios and the alignment of the businesses.

LESSONS LEARNED

This short workshop demonstrated the value of scenarios in providing a range of mental models based on differing assumptions – in this case, about globalization and technology. Although the scenarios were presented as describing 2020, the discussion quickly established that the business units had different default scenarios and tacit assumptions about the world. This recognition allowed them and the board to recognize synergies and dissonances, and to start the process of divestment.

Lessons learned and conclusions

This section summarizes the main points that emerge from the case studies. Many of these points are common across the range of applications, timescales and techniques. The conclusions summarize not only Part IV but the lessons for managers from the three earlier parts as well.

THE SCENARIO-DEVELOPMENT PROCESS

- It may not be necessary to develop scenarios: discussion of existing ones may provide the desired framework for discussion and decision (Section IV.8, "A trading group").

- Take the time and effort to ensure all team members are familiar with the process (Section IV.7, "Healthcare 2010" and Section IV.5, "Software for collaborative working").

- Decide on the desired outcome: whether a set of scenarios should be for discussion (Section IV.3, "New car distribution") or decision (Section IV.1, "A study in Turkey") or dialogue between industry players (Section IV.4, "Reframing industry boundaries").

- Ensure there is a wide range of input (Section IV.1, "A study in Turkey", Section IV.7, "Healthcare 2010" and Section IV.4, "Reframing industry boundaries".

- Include "unbelievable" scenarios (Section IV.2, "New energy environment").

268

- Do not be content with the first set of scenarios created (Section IV.6, "Foresight into insight").

SCENARIOS INTO ACTION

- Short workshops based on scenarios created earlier can be very effective at creating focus on the issues leading to their resolution (Section IV.8, "A trading group").

- A framework for action – an owning group or a planning framework – is necessary for action (Section IV.6, "Foresight into insight" and Section IV.2, "New energy environment").

- The support of the CEO is not enough to guarantee adoption (Section IV.6, "Foresight into insight").

- Even a short study can capture enough input to be helpful to management in decision making (Section IV.1, "A study in Turkey").

- Scenarios are used to inform decisions that are expected to be needed, by rehearsal (Section IV.2, "New energy environment").

- It may be possible to involve all the people who need to act in the scenario dialogue (Section IV.4, "Reframing industry boundaries" and Section IV.5, "Software for collaborative working").

- Otherwise, a focus on tools for communication of the scenarios is essential, both in terms of content and format (Section IV.6, "Foresight into insight").

- Scenarios travel best with those familiar with their source, however good the documentation, especially if follow-up action is required (Section IV.7, "Healthcare 2010").

- Synthetic futures, derived after the creation of scenarios, are useful in setting action plans (Section IV.7, "Healthcare 2010"), or it may be better to use challenges as the basis for action planning (Section IV.6, "Foresight into insight").

- "Unbelievable" scenarios may well transpire (Section IV.2, "New energy environment").

- At least some of the changes imagined in scenarios will happen faster than expected (Section IV.5, "Software for collaborative working").

- Most of the case studies emphasize that vision is an important element of scenarios that enables action.

CONCLUSIONS

In the last decade, the use of scenarios has changed from being considered part of corporate planning to part of strategic management. As organizations try to become nimble by empowering their staff, it becomes ever more important to ensure that the vision is shared to give coherence to actions. While the world is a complex and chaotic place, models of the world represented through scenario stories are frameworks that work at enabling people to relate, communicate and act.

Kees van der Heijden et al. (2002) argue that scenarios give managers a sixth sense: they believe that having a view forward allows managers to drive their organizations better, rather than driving with a historical, or rear view mirror, perspective.